YOUTUBE
SUPERSTARS

MAX AND MEI'S EPIC JOURNEY TO YOUTUBE STARDOM. . .

AND HOW YOU CAN GO VIRAL TOO.

CONTENTS

WELCOME TO THE YOUTUBE UNIVERSE

Max sat in his room, surrounded by posters of his favorite video game characters, a headset resting on his desk, and his gaming console humming softly in the background. He scrolled through his YouTube feed, watching his favorite personalities effortlessly rack up views and subscribers. As he clicked on a tutorial video on how to start a YouTube channel, he couldn't help but feel overwhelmed by the sheer amount of information.

"How am I supposed to compete with all these other gamers?" Max muttered. He knew how to set up a YouTube channel and upload videos, but he had no idea how to attract the numbers needed to turn his passion into a successful business.

Meanwhile, across town, Mei sat in front of her vanity mirror, brushes and colors spread before her like a painter's palette. She stared at her reflection, heart fluttering at the thought of starting her own makeup YouTube channel. She had always loved transforming faces with her artistry, but the idea of putting herself out there for the world to see was intimidating.

"I don't even know where to begin," Mei whispered to her reflection, uncertainty clouding her eyes. She had watched countless makeup tutorials on YouTube, marveling at the talent and creativity of the beauty community, but the thought of joining their ranks felt like an impossible feat.

As Max pondered strategies to grow his channel and Mei wrestled with the idea of taking the first step into the YouTube world, little did they know that their paths were about to intersect in ways that would change the course of their YouTube journeys forever.

The stage was set, the journey ahead promising both challenges and triumphs for these aspiring YouTubers. It was a world of endless possibilities, where success was just a click away. And with determination in their hearts and dreams in their eyes, Max and Mei were ready to embark on their quest for viral success.

There was just one problem.

How on earth were they going to do that?

PART 1: FINDING YOUR NICHE

In which our intrepid heroes—armed with their wits, their dreams, and some dangerously sugary snacks—embark on a grand search for the perfect YouTube channel.

1
NICHE? NICE!

Make your channel be about something

The aroma of freshly brewed coffee filled the air as Mei settled into a cozy corner of the bustling café, her notebook spread open in front of her. She absentmindedly twirled a pen in her fingers, sketching out makeup ideas for her next project. The hum of conversation and the clinking of cups provided a comforting background noise, but Mei was lost in her thoughts.

Max entered the café, scanning the room for an empty seat. Spotting Mei's table with an extra chair, he approached hesitantly. "Excuse me, mind if I sit here? The place is packed."

Mei looked up, momentarily startled. "Sure," she said with a smile. "It's pretty busy today."

Max settled into the chair, placing his laptop on the table. "Thanks. I'm Max, by the way."

"Mei," she replied, pronouncing the word like *May*. She returned to her notebook, but after a moment curiosity got the better of her. "What are you working on?"

Max spun his screen, proudly showing a list of video ideas. "Brainstorming my YouTube channel."

"No way!" said Mei, eyes wide. "I'm working on a YouTube channel too, but for makeup tutorials." She bit her lip. "I'm, ah... struggling to work out where to start. Do you know?"

Max gave a huge grin. "Nope!" he proclaimed loudly. "Flying by the seat of my pants."

At Mei's snort, he continued, "Well, sort of. I figure the first step should be to work out the type of content I want."

Mei clutched her head in her hands. "Tell me about it. That's where I'm at too. You'd think just 'make-up videos' would be enough, but there are so many different things within there I could be doing!"

She looked up. "What about you?"

"Mine'll be something with gaming," he said, looking over his list. He pulled a face. "Problem is, how do I stand out from the crowd?"

Mei nodded. "Same. I love makeup, but there are so many beauty channels. I need a niche."

"Nice?"

"Niche."

At his blank expression, she bit her lip. "Sorry, I use big words sometimes. A niche is something specific that you're an expert in. It's basically what you were just saying—trying to do everything about make-up will just get me lost in the crowd. But if I can get known for one specific thing, I'll stand out." She pursed her lips at a thought. "Makeup for cosplayers, maybe?"

"That sounds awesome!" Max said. "I'd love to see that!"

He grimaced, trying to work out what his niche might be. Eventually, he tapped at his screen. "Maybe... uh, if you're okay with it... we can help each other out? You know, bounce ideas off each other?"

Mei grinned. "I'd like that." She picked up her iced chocolate, extending it for a clink. Hurriedly, Max grabbed a glass of water.

"To working out this whole YouTube thing," Mei said.

"Screw that!" Max exclaimed. "To going viral and becoming superstars!"

With a laugh they clinked glasses, unaware that they'd both just started a journey that would change their lives and their channels forever.

2
RESEARCH, SNACKS, REPEAT

Personal passion + market research = unique niche

Three days later, Mei and Max met at the local library. Mei had suggested the location—she visited regularly. Max had agreed only grudgingly.

Libraries were an intimidating place for Max, who hadn't visited one since a series of mandatory school trips several years ago. But Mei had convinced him it would be a good place to study and talk, and as he gazed around, he realized she was right. The room before them was a quiet place with vast resources perfect for their research session. The scent of old books and polished wood filled the air, creating a serene atmosphere.

They settled at a large wooden table, surrounded by stacks of books with their laptops open, ready to dive into their brainstorming session.

Mei pulled out a pencil and notebook. There were sketches and ideas all over the cover. "Alright, let's get started. I was thinking we should list out what we love and what we're good at."

"This is to find our… *niche*, right?"

She beamed a smile. "Right! You remembered."

"Of course!" Max said indignantly. On the inside though, he breathed a sigh of relief—he'd been practicing the word all day.

Mei smiled. "For me, it's definitely got to be something about makeup and creativity," she said. "I think I'm onto something with the cosplay idea. I've always loved transforming people into different characters, especially for plays and events."

She jotted the words *makeup*, and *creativity*, down on her pad.

Max leaned back, thinking about what his own unique angle could be. "I mean, I could just pick games that I really like to play, but which people haven't done a lot of videos about. That's getting harder and harder, though."

Mei nodded. "Yeah, true. Remember, a niche doesn't have to be something product related. It could be *how* you play the games, or who your audience is, or even a style of video. MrBeast's niche is spending buttloads of money to do crazy things!"

Max laughed out loud, earning a *shush* from the librarian. He tapped at the table in thought. "But you do give me an idea."

Mei raised an eyebrow.

Max laughed again, but bit his lip at the librarian's glare. "Nothing to do with spending non-existent money," he whispered. "But, what if my audience were newbies? I'm great at explaining games to friends, maybe I could focus on that? You know, show my gameplay, but then explain what I'm doing while I'm doing it."

"Great idea!" Mei wrote it down. "It would attract lots of new viewers." Her pen tapped against her teeth. "I'm wondering if I should do makeup tutorials that *integrate* cosplay, instead of just straight cosplay? I could show how to create looks inspired by games and movies?"

Max nodded enthusiastically. "That's brilliant! It opens you up to a wider audience than just straight dress-ups."

They began throwing ideas at each other, bouncing suggestions back and forth. Mei wrote everything down in her book.

"We should also research what's already out there," suggested Max. "See what successful channels are doing. Find gaps we can fill."

Mei agreed. "I'll look up cosplay makeup tutorials and see what's trending," she said, tapping into her laptop. "You check out gaming channels and see what's popular."

For the next couple of hours they immersed themselves in 'research,' though honestly, it didn't really feel like that. They were just checking out things they loved! They watched videos, read articles, and Mei took notes on what worked and what didn't. Max discovered that while there were many gaming channels—he even subscribed to a bunch!—few really focused on helping out beginners. Mei found that while there were cosplay makeup tutorials, many were focused on full transformations, not the *inspired by* makeovers she hoped to offer.

Taking a break toward the end of their session, Max snapped a line from a block of chocolate, popping it into his mouth.

"We're not supposed to eat in here," Mei chided.

"Want some?" he asked, offering the bar.

"You know it!" She snatched it from him, and they chuckled as they ate contraband together.

Max eyed Mei's notes while they did. Mouth full, he asked, "*If phony dersh shum way we cud ashk shummone 'bout dis.*"

Mei pulled a face. "*What?*"

He swallowed. "If only there was some way we could ask someone about all of this."

"Ah." Mei pondered the question. "Well, I mean there are a heap of YouTube videos and books on how to start YouTube channels. That's what we're doing now..."

"The videos are kind of cool," Max shrugged. "But books aren't really my thing."

She raised an eyebrow. "Yeah, I've noticed. You haven't taken a single note since we've been here."

Max tapped his head with a mischievous grin. "It's all up here. This thing's like a steel vault."

"More like a leaky, rusting bucket," Mei muttered.

"What was that?"

Mei coughed. "Come to think of it, I think I might know someone that can help." She sat up straighter. "A friend mentioned at a party once they knew someone with a YouTube channel. Want me to try and get in touch?"

Now Max sat up too. "That would be awesome! Talking to someone in person would be so helpful. Reckon you could do it?"

"I'll try my best," she replied. Her lips formed the same mischievous grin Max had just thrown at her. "Reckon you could take some notes?"

Max pulled a face. "Urgh. Can't we just record it instead?"

3
LOVE IS IN THE AIR?

Look for the overlap between what you love and others love to watch

A week after their research session at the library, Mei and Max huddled together in Mei's living room, drinking steaming mugs of hot chocolate that her mom had made them.

"When's the meeting?" Max asked.

"Ten minutes," replied Mei. "Jimmy has this awesome channel that talks about collectibles. It's got over twenty thousand subscribers."

"Oh man. I wish!" said Max.

"I know, right? Anyway, let's move to my bedroom and set up."

Mei's mom poked her head in from the kitchen. "Uh-uh, sorry kids," she said, tying her hair up with a green kerchief. "No boyfriends in the bedroom. House rule."

Max turned to Mei. Mei turned bright red. "MOM! It's not like that!"

"Oh. I thought all that YouTube stuff was just an excuse for you two to get all cuddly."

Mei buried her face in her hands. "I'll just crawl into a corner and die now," she muttered from between her fingers.

Max couldn't help but laugh. His mom would have totally done the same. *Parents these days. Sheesh.*

Mei's mom asked them to take their video chat in the lounge room even though 'she totally believed that the Facechat thingy was real and not an excuse for Mei to hang out with Max who seemed like a nice young boy.' Mei had gone even more red at that!

They were saved when Mei's phone rang. She grabbed it hastily to accept a chat.

"Hey guys!" A cheery face appeared on the screen. "I'm Jimmy, a friend of Emily's. She told me you two are looking to start your own YouTube channels?"

Mei's mom, who had been standing behind them, cocked her head. "Well, I'll be," she murmured. Patting her daughter briefly on the shoulder, she walked back into the kitchen.

"Ah... yeah," Max muttered, trying to get his head back in the game. "I'm Max, nice to meet you. We've been trying to figure out how to stand out. We have some ideas, but aren't sure how to refine them."

Jimmy smiled. "Alright, let's dive in. The key is to find what you love, but also what others love to watch. Look for the overlap."

Mei leaned forward. With her mom gone, she'd lost several shades of red. "So, it's about balancing passion with demand?"

"Careful your mom doesn't hear you," Max joked under his breath. Mei elbowed him.

"Exactly," Jimmy replied, missing the exchange. "Your passion will drive your content, but understanding what the audience wants will help you grow. For instance, Max, I *love* the idea of teaching noobs how to play games. But what happens then? You'll lose them if you don't understand what they want next. Do stuff for beginners, but also more advanced vids for when those beginners become experts. That's your sweet spot."

His pointed to Mei. "Same with you. Think about what your audience might want, and where it crosses with what you want. Cosplay inspired videos are great, but they're useless if no-one wants to be that character. Follow the trends. Watch the latest movies, play the latest games, and do makeup inspired by the coolest characters you see. You'll be tapping into a niche market that craves new ideas."

Max and Mei nodded, absorbing the advice. Jimmy continued, "Research is crucial. Look at what's trending, but also identify gaps. Consistency and engagement are your best friends. Always interact with your audience and ask for feedback."

They talked more about their ideas—Jimmy was busy, but he could spare some time for friends of friends. "You know, the two of you can do some pretty awesome crossovers once you get going a bit," he said as they neared the end of their call. "Never forget the power of cross promotion."

He looked at Mei. "Consider doing cosplay inspired makeup of characters from the games that Max talks about." Now he turned to Max. "And not only could you do shout-outs when she does, but you could even cosplay as you game occasionally! Get Mei to do your makeup – it's an easy way to attract and share audiences."

They both nodded enthusiastically. Jimmy signed off, promising to give them both shout outs on his own channel once they got going, too. Mei's hands were a blur as she wrote down the key points of everything they'd gone over.

Max just coughed. He'd been so distracted by Mei's mom that he'd forgotten to record it. "Um, mind if I borrow those notes when you're done?"

4
MIND THE GAPS

Identify gaps in existing YouTube content

A few days later, Mei and Max met at a local community center. The building's primary purpose was as a large, multi-function hall where people much fitter than either of them did gymnastics and Zumba, but it also featured a super chill youth lounge—a welcoming space filled with bean bags, colorful posters and computers available for use.

The room buzzed with the chatter of other teens avoiding strenuous workouts. They found a quiet corner to focus on their research.

"Alright," Max began, settling into a bean bag and opening YouTube on his laptop. "Jimmy said to do research, so let's have a look what's out there. I'll start with game tutorial channels and see what's popular."

Mei nodded, taking a seat next to him and pulling up YouTube on her own device. "I'll do the same for cosplay makeup tutorials. I want to see what's trending and any gaps we can fill."

For the next hour, they immersed themselves in the world of YouTube, exploring channels and noting their findings. Max watched videos from popular gamers, noting the high production values and engaging storytelling. "Look at this," he said, turning his laptop towards Mei. "This channel dives deep into game lore and mechanics, but it's not newbie friendly. Even I don't understand some of the terms. There's a niche there."

Mei glanced at the screen, intrigued. "That's a great angle. Indie games have passionate communities that are often underserved. You could become the go-to guy for those games."

Max smiled, jotting down notes. "Exactly. Now, let's see what you've found."

Mei turned her laptop to show a series of popular cosplay makeup tutorials. "This channel does 'inspiration' makeup as well, but it's still for people already in the community. There's not much out there for people that just want to add a touch of Zelda or whatever to their look. That could be my angle—accessible, game inspired makeup."

Max nodded. "I like that. It's unique and will attract a specific audience looking for something different. Plus, you could collaborate with cosplay communities to expand your reach."

Mei's eyes lit up. "That's a fantastic idea. I could even do live streams where I create looks based on audience requests. It would make the channel interactive, which is a good thing, right?

Max nodded. "Totally."

They continued their research, occasionally sharing interesting finds with each other. Max discovered a few smaller channels that did something called overexplaining, which was where they played a game very slowly, stopping to show inventory screens and talking through every single thing they did. It was super interesting—even a veteran like Max could pick up tips—but they all lacked consistency and polish. "Regular uploads with high-quality production for the win! I think it would fill a significant gap."

Mei nodded, grinning. "And I'll keep building my brand with my own spin on makeup. I could do occasional full cosplay stuff as well—reinforce the fact that I know what I'm doing. If we stay consistent and level up our content, we'll totally stand out."

"So, What's next?" Max asked at the end of their session. He stood and stretched. "More research?"

Mei scrunched up her face. "I feel like we've got a nice handle on something that each of us can do to make our channel unique." She bit her lip and swallowed. "I guess now we just... do it?"

5
TO SWIM, YOU'VE GOT TO GET WET

Publish that first video!

Mei was in her bedroom, which she had transformed into a mini studio for the day. Posters of her favorite characters adorned the walls, and her phone was set up on a makeshift tripod crafted from a stack of books. She checked the angle, ensuring the frame captured her face and her colorful backdrop. Taking a deep breath, she smiled at the camera. "Hey every-"

Knock, knock.

"Who is it?"

Mei's mom poked her head around the door. "I'm heading to the beach. Want to join?"

"Sorry Mom, doing YouTube stuff."

One eyebrow raised. "Oh. So, you're actually doing this?"

Mei rolled her eyes. "Yes, Mom."

"Oh. Anything I can do to help?"

"Thanks Mom. Actually, a quiet house would be awesome. Go enjoy the beach."

"Oh, good luck honey! I'll have a swim for you."

The door clicked shut. Mei took another deep breath, centering herself, then started again. "Hey everyone! Today, we're doing makeup inspired by my favorite game, Breath of the Wild. Let's get started!"

Meanwhile, Max was in his bedroom, surrounded by shelves filled with video games and memorabilia. He propped his phone against a stack of game cases, checking to ensure it captured his face and his notes. Pressing record, he faced the camera with a confident grin. "Hey gamers! Today, we're doing a full walkthrough for beginners. I'll show you everything you need to know to get started—step by step!"

In separate rooms in separate houses, Max and Mei spoke passionately about something they loved. It was a beautiful day, and they could have been at the beach, or the arcade, or a million other places, but instead they were exactly where they wanted to be. There were no high-quality microphones or elaborate lighting setups—just their phones and their passion. There was background noise, interruptions and stumbles; their content wasn't perfect. But it was a start.

Later that week, they met again at the community center's youth lounge to compare results. Mei's face lit as she saw Max approaching with his laptop. "How did it go?" she asked eagerly.

"It was awesome," Max replied, setting up his laptop. "I think we've got some great content. Let's see what we've got."

They sat together, watching each other's videos. Mei's makeup tutorial was vibrant and engaging, her enthusiasm infectious. Max's overexplained videos were detailed and captivating, his passion drawing viewers into the game.

"This is amazing," Mei said, pulling out a pad of paper. "How are the views?"

Max grimaced. "Excluding family and friends? Pretty terrible"

Mei shrugged. "Me too. I got like three subs, and I'm pretty sure one is a bot."

He nodded his head in commiseration. "It's a start. We just need to keep refining our content."

Mei began diligently jotting down something in her notebook, her pen moving rapidly across the pages.

Mei glanced up from her notes and noticed Max staring into space, his notebook untouched beside him. "Still not taking any notes?" she asked, raising an eyebrow.

Max shifted uncomfortably in his seat and scratched the back of his head. "Uh, it's not really my thing," he admitted, looking a bit embarrassed.

Mei chuckled. "Not your thing? Max, how are you going to remember all these great ideas? Also, I *know* you forgot to record our chat with Jimmy."

Max shrugged, a sheepish grin on his face. "I guess I'm more of a 'live in the moment' kind of guy. Besides, you're so good at it."

Mei rolled her eyes. "Well, we need to have a reference for the future. How about this? I'll take notes for both of us. That way, we'll have everything written down, and you can keep living in the moment."

Max's eyes lit up. "Really? That would be awesome. You're the best!"

Mei smiled and nodded. "Alright, deal. But you owe me a smoothie."

Max laughed. "Deal! I'll take you to this amazing beach café I know—anything for my amazing note-taking partner."

MEI'S NOTES:
FINDING YOUR NICHE

Do what you love

The more you're into something, the better your content will be. If you're hyped about it, your viewers will be too - whether it's makeup, gaming, or whatever!

Balance passion with what people want

Sure, you love it, but you've gotta figure out what your audience wants to see too. Like Jimmy said, the sweet spot is where your interests and their interests overlap.

Mash up your interests

Combining things you love makes you stand out. Like, why just do makeup when I can add cosplay? Max is all about making gaming tutorials for noobs - it's his unique spin.

Research is Everything
Before you get too far ahead, check out what's already out there. We spent hours watching videos (okay, fun research!), and we figured out what's missing in the mix.

Ask for help
There's always someone who's been there before. Talking to Jimmy was super helpful. If you know someone with experience, pick their brain!

Keep it real
Don't fake it. People can tell. Just be yourself, and your audience will appreciate that.

If research feels fun, you're doing it right
Honestly, if researching feels like just watching more of what you love, then you're definitely on the right path.

And don't forget
Max owes me a large mango smoothie. I'm holding him to that!

PART 2: EQUIPMENT ESSENTIALS

In which our intrepid heroes learn that a dazzling glow and crystal-clear sound can be coaxed from even the humblest of gadgets, all while nursing a mild case of brain freeze.

6
PIXELATED PROBLEMS, CLEAR SOLUTIONS

Better equipment will improve video and sound quality

Max had just finished editing his latest overexplained gaming video. Pumped to see it on the big screen, he called his family into the living room, eager to show off his hard work.

The video started, and at first, everything seemed fine. The gameplay footage was crisp, thanks to the new video card he'd saved up for all summer. But as soon as he saw himself in the corner of the screen, his smile faded. On his PC monitor, his facecam had looked sharp, but blown up on the family TV? It was grainy, blurry—honestly, a mess.

Then came the audio. His voice crackled like an old radio, barely audible over the background noise of his room. At one point, a plane flew overhead, and for a full minute, his lips were moving, but there was zero sound. Max cringed, pausing the video. "This... isn't it," he muttered under his breath. His family reassured him it was fine, but Max couldn't shake the disappointment as he slunk out of the room, frustrated.

Across town, Mei was going through her own struggle. She pressed play on her latest makeup tutorial, excited to see her hard work on her family's big TV. Her bedroom, usually a creative haven with makeup palettes and posters everywhere, suddenly didn't seem so perfect.

The video played, but it was nothing like she'd imagined. Her vibrant makeup looked dull and flat on the big screen, the colors completely off. Shadows from her desk lamp turned her careful detailing into a blur. "Ugh," she groaned, pausing the video. The lighting was wrecking everything. All those hours perfecting the cosplay look, and now it felt like it didn't even matter.

Later that evening, Max and Mei vented to each other over text:

Max: Just watched my video on the TV… it SUCKS. Video was blurry, and the sound was even worse. I srsly might give up.

Mei: Hang in there! I'm having the same issue. My makeup tutorial looks awful on the big screen—lighting ruined everything. We'll fix it, though. Want to meet up and figure this out together?

The next day, Max and Mei met up at the community center's youth lounge, determined to fix their video problems. Laptops and notepads in front of them, Max opened his laptop first and played the footage. "Look at this," he groaned. "All that editing work, and it's wasted because the video looks grainy and the sound is a mess."

Mei winced at the muffled audio and pixelated screen. "Yeah, that's rough. But check this out." She pulled up her own video. "The lighting is a disaster. Shadows everywhere, and the colors are totally washed out. It looks like I filmed it in a basement."

They exchanged glances, both realizing the same thing.

"We need better equipment," Mei said, tapping her fingers on the table. "No way around it."

Max grimaced. "Yeah. We just don't look professional."

Mei snorted. "You're never professional!"

When Max opened his mouth to protest, she held up his hands. "*Joking.* I know exactly what you mean. And I agree. Our phones and desk lamps were fine to get started. But we need to level up."

It was depressing, but also exciting. Their videos were awful, but they knew *why* – and it was an easy fix! It wasn't that the content was boring. Their ideas still had merit! It was just that their equipment hadn't done the ideas justice.

"Maybe with better lighting, we can each get more than three subscribers," Max joked.

"I'd settle for four," Mei said. "…Million."

They laughed, then dived into research.

7
LIGHTS, CAMERA... ZUMBA?

Light and sound are important
Research essential tools

The following afternoon, Max and Mei met at the community center's youth lounge, intending to brainstorm and research in a quiet and familiar location—they still weren't allowed in Mei's bedroom, and Max's house was far too noisy.

Walking through the door, however, they found the area crowded. All the chairs and beanbags were taken, and most of the floor space and tabletops were occupied too. It was crowded, noisy and not the calm, quiet atmosphere they'd been hoping to research new equipment in.

"What's going on?" asked Mei, looking around with dismay.

One of the boys waved. "Max, *duuude.* Great recommendation! Hope you don't mind—I told some friends."

Sheepishly, Max rubbed the back of his head. "I, ah, might have told a couple of people about the center. Thought it was a fun place to hang out."

Mei gave him side eye. "Remind me never to ask you to keep a secret." She looked around, then sighed. "Where next? We obviously can't work here."

They wandered through the center, looking for a spare table. The small indoor aqua-aerobics area was out—not only was the humidity terrible for their laptops, but the noise of twenty grannies splashing and chatting was almost deafening.

They were pleasantly surprised, however, to find that the huge community hall, usually reserved for Zumba, was empty. Max took one look at the huge shed with its vaulted ceiling and polished wooden floor, then marched straight to the middle and sat, grinning.

With a sigh, Mei followed him, sitting beside him in the cavernous space. "There are like, chairs and stuff on the sidelines, you know."

"Yeah, I know," Max said. "But this is way more fun. Besides, this way we can see anyone sneaking up to spy on our secret plans."

"Researching better lights and cameras isn't exactly super secret."

"You say that now. But wait until we're YouTube superstars. Then everyone will be wanting to know our gear."

Mei just rolled her eyes, pulling out her laptop.

Max began searching for information on lighting equipment. He had no idea where to start with his own issues, but he did know what to do about Mei's. "Alright, let's see what we can find about improving lighting. I read that good lighting can totally change the way a video looks—something about making it even and consistent."

Mei nodded, pulling out her own laptop. "And we need to find ways to improve your sound quality. I think maybe an external mic?"

As they dove into their research, Max stumbled on an article about improving video quality. "Hey, check this out," he said, scrolling down. "There's something called a three-point lighting setup—seems like it's the go-to for making videos look professional."

Mei leaned over, squinting at the screen. "Three-point lighting? Sounds fancy."

Max grinned. "Not really! It's just lights that can fix the shadows. Make everything look clear."

He skimmed the article and leaned in to explain. "Okay, picture this—you're doing one of your makeup tutorials, right? The key light is like the spotlight on your face. It's the main light, and it shows off all the cool details you worked on, like your makeup."

Mei nodded, already visualizing it.

"Then," Max continued, "you've got the fill light. It's opposite the key light and softens any harsh shadows. You know how sometimes you get weird dark spots on your face when the light's only coming from one side? The fill light evens that out, so your makeup doesn't look patchy."

Mei bit her lip. "Okay, makes sense. And the backlight?"

Max pointed to his screen. "That's the light behind you. It helps you stand out from the background. Like, instead of looking flat or blending into your room, it gives your videos more depth and makes you pop."

Mei's eyes lit up. "I'm gonna so look like a pro! And the talking head part of your gaming videos!"

Max tilted his head at that. She was right.

They moved on, and soon Mei was deep into reading about different types of microphones. "Okay, so it looks like lavalier mics are perfect for makeup tutorials. I can clip one onto my clothes, and it'll pick up my voice clearly without catching all the background noise—like when my mom decides to vacuum mid-video," she said with a laugh.

Max glanced over. "Sounds great! Would that work for my stuff too?"

Mei scrolled through the article. "For your gaming videos, a shotgun mic would be better. It can focus directly on your voice and block out the background stuff—like the clacking of your keyboard or, you know, planes flying overhead during your recording," she laughed.

Max winced at the memory. "Yeah, I could really use that."

They didn't stop there. Mei found a section on camera stability and sighed. "I'll need a tripod too—no one wants to see shaky footage, it's super distracting."

Max nodded. "Yeah, that'll help a lot with your tutorials. For me, too." He swiveled his screen toward her. There's also video resolution. Our webcams aren't good enough. We need at *least* 1080p for our videos to look sharp. Something with a good framerate will make everything look smoother, too."

Mei groaned. "New lights. Tripod. Microphones and cameras. Have we done anything right so far?"

Max punched her lightly in the arm. "Of course we have. We've started. That puts us ahead of like, 99% of the population. Everything else is just learning on the job."

A troupe of grannies wearing neon spandex walked into the room, chattering about their upcoming Zumba class. Max and Mei got to their feet.

"I think that's our cue to get out of here," said Max. "Shopping trip next Saturday?"

Mei nodded, flashing her notebook. "I took notes... and you still owe me that smoothie."

8
BIG DREAMS, EMPTY WALLETS

Look for capability, not brands

Though they had originally planned to go shopping on Saturday, after some thought Max and Mei decided to hit the electronics store weekday afternoon, instead. The store was usually quiet in the afternoons, and they hoped the assistants would have time to chat and give advice.

They walked in sipping smoothies, which were totally not as good as the ones Max wanted to show Mei at his mystery beach café. They walked back out 30 seconds later, realizing an electronics store wasn't an ideal place to be sipping liquid machine death, and then returned a minute after that groaning about brain freeze.

They were greeted by a tech lover's paradise of cool gadgets and items, heading straight to the video and lighting section, which they hoped would hold the majority of their wishlist.

A store assistant, adjusting display models, looked up and smiled at their approach. "Hi there! I'm Jake. Can I help you?"

Max stepped forward. "Yeah, we're trying to improve our YouTube videos and need advice on equipment. We've done some research and are interested in three-point lighting setups and microphones—both lavalier and shotgun mics."

Jake's eyes lit up. "Ah, good call! For three-point lighting, I'd suggest starting with a ring light and softboxes. The ring light works great as your main light—it's a ring of LEDs, and you can position your camera right in the center. Perfect for close-ups, like makeup tutorials or vlogs. Then, softboxes for your fill and backlight. They'll smooth out any harsh shadows and give everything a professional look."

He gestured toward the microphone section, leading them down an aisle. "As for sound, you're on the right track. Lav mics are perfect for clear, hands-free audio. They pick up your voice without the background noise. And shotgun mics? Spot on for directional sound, especially if you're doing commentary or gameplay—cuts out the extra noise."

He picked up a sleek, black lavalier mic, holding it up with a grin. "This one here is my personal favorite. Super reliable, great clarity. It'll definitely up your audio game."

When Max looked at the price tag, his excitement dimmed.

"Umm," Max said, scratching the back of his head. "You don't happen to have anything cheaper, do you?"

"Sure!" Jake plucked another microphone from the shelf. "This is almost as good, and half the price!"

"Umm… cheaper?"

Jake's face slumped. Squatting down, he pulled a dusty plastic box from the bottom shelf. "This is our absolute budget model. Honestly, your phones would be better. And I bet you can't afford it either, can you?"

Mei's face scrunched up. "Sorry," she whispered. "We're kinda broke right now. Just starting out."

Instead of being disappointed, Jake broke into a grin. "Eh, it's fine—I can't afford half this stuff either. Also, my boss is a total ass. He doesn't deserve the money."

He motioned them closer. "When you have the money, jump online—there's plenty of cheap foreign brands that do just as good a job as Sony or Sennheiser. Just make sure you read all the reviews, and get something with a good star rating."

He leaned back. "Until then, have you considered DIY?"

Mei and Max's blank looks were all he needed to continue. "For lighting, use desk lamps with soft white bulbs. You can then diffuse the light with fabric or wax paper. It's not as good as a softbox, but it works well enough."

Mei perked up. "What about the microphones? Any ideas?"

Jake grinned. "Oh yeah, start with a basic lavalier mic. You're gonna have to drop a little cash, but I've seen some decent ones on Amazon for under fifty. Way better than using your phone's built-in mic, trust me. Plus, make yourself a DIY sound shield with cardboard and foam to cut down background noise. The shotgun mic will cost more, but you can work up to that. The lav mic'll hold you over."

Mei's eyes lit up. "Fifty bucks? We can definitely swing that. You're a lifesaver, thanks!"

Jake nodded. "No problem at all. Start small, upgrade as your channel grows. And don't forget camera stability—a tripod will change your life compared to handheld."

Max and Mei wandered around the store, their eyes drawn to the high-end equipment they dreamt of owning. Jake even let them mess around with some of the fancy cameras.

"You want to shoot in at least 1080p," Jake said, pointing to a sleek model. "Full HD. If you've got the gear for it, 4K is next-level. Though..." He looked at Mei. "Pass me your phone."

Mei handed it over, curious. As Max started checking out some green screens, Jake scrolled through her phone's settings. "Nice! Your phone can handle 4K already. It'll eat up storage, but the quality is worth it." He quickly adjusted her resolution. "Future-proofing your content for all those fancy new TVs and monitors coming out."

Mei blinked. "Wait, what? I can shoot in 4K already?"

Jake winked. "You bet. Perfect for those makeup tutorials. Really lets the details shine." He winked. "Don't mind the odd bit of eyeliner myself, when I go out. Really makes the eyes pop."

Mei burst out laughing. "You've got great eyes, Jake."

He grinned. "And just for that, I'll give you another tip." He glanced at Max, who had progressed to flossing on what looked like a beach in the Bahamas. "We have time."

Mei covered her face. "OMG, I'm so embarrassed."

Jake chuckled. "Tell me about it. Flossing? That's so 2016."

"Fortnite forever!" Max shouted in protest.

Jake turned back to Mei's phone, his expression changing. "Oh, bummer. Your phone doesn't have this yet."

"What is it?" Mei asked, curious.

"Not a deal-breaker, but when you upgrade, make sure your new camera can handle different frame rates—24fps for cinematic, 30fps for regular video, and 60fps for smooth, action-packed stuff." He glanced up at her confused look. "FPS stands for frames per second. Think of it like a flipbook—the more frames you have, the smoother the video looks."

Jake shrugged. "Most YouTube videos are shot at 30fps. It's a nice balance between smooth motion and storage space."

Mei beamed. "You've amazing. Thank you!"

Jake grinned. "Just remember me when you're famous."

From across the store, where Max was now dramatically pretending to surf in front of the greenscreen, he shouted, "Will do!"

9
FROM BLURRY TO BRILLIANT

You don't need a lot of money

Several days later, Max sat in his room, the soft glow of his desk lamp casting long shadows as he tinkered with his latest project: a DIY sound shield. Armed with a cardboard box lined with foam he'd scavenged from the garage, he carefully placed his phone's mic inside, praying it would cut out background noise.

He winced, thinking about the awful moment in his last video when a plane had roared overhead, leaving him mute for a full minute. This time, though, he had a plan. After checking flight paths online (because of course he did), Max realized he had a solid two-hour window each afternoon where no planes would disrupt his masterpiece. To be extra safe, he'd closed his window and hung up thick blankets on the walls to dampen any rogue sounds. His mattress was now awkwardly wedged against the door, blocking kitchen noises. Sure, he'd have to rebuild his bed later, but what was a little inconvenience for future fame?

Meanwhile, across town, Mei was in full MacGyver mode,

having spent the last few days piecing together her own three-point lighting system using 'borrowed' items from around the house. It wasn't like her mom would miss that desk lamp, would she?

Using her totally-not-my-mom's desk lamp as the key light, Mei positioned it in front of her to highlight her face. The lounge room's floor lamp? Totally-not-missing, now draped in a white pillowcase and placed off to one side as the fill light. Instantly, she noticed it made her look way less like a Halloween shadow puppet.

Finally, she placed a small bedside lamp (finally, something she actually owned) behind her as a backlight, now wrapped in a piece of wax paper from the kitchen. It softened the glow just enough to give her that professional YouTuber vibe without making her room look like a film set.

Sitting back to watch her latest makeup tutorial, she couldn't help but grin. The lighting was way more even, the colors popping off the screen. "Okay, that's a serious upgrade," she muttered, pleased with the vibrant results. Now, if only she could figure out what to do with the background. Max's greenscreen antics had given her some ideas. Should she go minimalist with a sheet or stick with the tidy-but-busy look of her room? She decided to experiment with both—if Max could floss on a beach in the Bahamas, she could figure this out too.

Later that afternoon, Max and Mei met up at a local park. The place bursting with life—kids racing around, cyclists whizzing by, and the smell of food trucks wafting through the air. It wasn't somewhere they could study, but it was totally somewhere they could hang and watch each other's videos, which was exactly why they were here. They plopped down on a bench beneath a sprawling oak tree, both buzzing with excitement.

Max went first, flipping his phone around to show Mei. "Okay, check this out. Remember that DIY sound shield? It actually worked!" He tapped play, the sound of his voice crisp and clear, a far cry from the echoey mess of his earlier attempts.

Mei's eyes widened as she listened. "This is a game-changer! You don't sound like you're talking from inside a cave anymore. It makes everything you say soooo much easier to follow. Huge upgrade!"

Max grinned. "Told ya! Now, let's see what you've got."

Mei opened her phone, playing her makeup tutorial. Max leaned in, squinting at the screen. "Whoa, Mei! Your makeup really pops now. The lighting's not just better, it's pro-level. The shadows are totally gone!"

They went back and forth, geeking out over the improvements. Max had nailed the audio, and Mei had cracked the lighting code. It was like they'd each leveled up their skills in the areas where the other was struggling.

Max turned to Mei, his brain racing. "Hey, what if we team up for our next videos? I help you with sound and you fix my lighting? We'll be unstoppable."

Mei grinned, already imagining the possibilities. "Deal! We'll create videos so epic, even MrBeast will be jealous."

Max laughed, pretending to look around. "Yeah, well, when he shows up offering you a million dollars to work with him, just remember—I found you first!"

MEI'S NOTES:
EQUIPMENT ESSENTIALS

Lighting is everything
OMG, lighting can *make or break* your video. I set up a DIY three-point lighting system in my room with lamps found around the house. Shadows? Gone! Colors? *Pop.* I can't believe how good even, consistent lighting makes everything look!

Three-point lighting is the way to go:

- Key Light (main light in front of you)
- Fill Light (opposite side to soften shadows)
- Backlight (behind you to add depth).

Backgrounds matter
A cluttered background can ruin an otherwise perfect video. Keep it simple and tidy, or go all out and use a green screen for extra creativity. Max gave me the idea, and now I'm considering using one for my next tutorial. It's time to level up!

Sound matters more than you think

People can forgive slightly bad visuals, but bad audio? Nope. I learned from Max that using an external mic like a lavalier (a tiny clip-on one) gives you much clearer sound, especially for makeup tutorials where I need to be close to the camera. If stuff further away, a shotgun mic is gold. Oh, and if you live in a noisy house (like me), consider filming when it's quiet (late at night or early mornings) or even sound-proofing your room with blankets.

DIY is your best friend

Can't afford expensive gear? Welcome to the club! You can totally hack your setup:

- Softboxes? *Pshh.* Desk lamps with soft bulbs and a piece of wax paper draped over them work just fine.
- Soundproofing? Max made a sound shield from cardboard and foam, and it cut out *so* much background noise. It's like leveling up your setup without spending the XP (aka, money).

Stability = pro-looking videos

Tripods are *essential.* Balancing your phone on a stack of books might work at first (guilty!), but a tripod makes such a difference. No one wants to watch shaky footage.

Shoot in 1080p or go home

Resolution: Aim for at least 1080p (Full HD) to keep everything clear. If your phone can handle it (thanks, Jake!), shoot in 4K. More clarity means more professional videos.

Frame Rate: Choose 30fps for most videos or 60fps if you're doing something high-energy (like Max and his gaming walk-throughs). Keep your vids smooth and professional, not like a jittery flipbook.

Start small, Dream big

You don't need to buy expensive gear right off the bat. Start with what you have, and improve your setup over time. With better lighting, sound, and camera work, we're going to *kill* it - but one upgrade at a time.

Get resourceful

Don't spend money unless you absolutely have to! Borrow gear, ask your local library if they have equipment you can use, or see if your friends have a camera lying around. Honestly, there's always a way to make it work without blowing your budget.

Get resourceful

Yes, I said it twice. It's that important!

PART 3: CREATING COMPELLING CONTENT

In which our intrepid heroes learn that crafting must-watch videos isn't just about fancy tickets or flashy tricks—but about weaving stories that dazzle, sincerity that wins hearts, and hooks that pull viewers in before they can even glance at the exit.

10
BEACHSIDE BRAINSTORM

Brainstorm, plan, tell a story.

It was time for Max to finally make good on his promise.

"The usual, sir?" asked a waiter.

Max held up two fingers. "Double it."

Two mango smoothies arrived shortly after, tall glasses frosted with condensation and filled to the brim with vibrant, golden liquid. Each was topped with a swirl of whipped cream and a slice of fresh mango perched on the rim.

The café they'd chosen was nestled along a bustling strip opposite the local beach, where surfers rode waves and the sun cast a warm, inviting glow. The street was a kaleidoscope of colors and sounds—cafés of every type packed side by side.

Mei took one sip of her smoothie and her eyes widened. "OMG, this is so good!" She sucked with such enthusiasm that she leaned back moments later, out of breath but utterly content.

"That's almost better than churros," she groaned.

"Churros?"

She raised an eyebrow. "I'll introduce you sometime. You'll see."

At the next table, three surfer girls chatted away, their beach-blonde hair still damp from the ocean. With glowing tans and easy laughter, they were enjoying their own smoothies almost as much as Mei. She found herself wondering what their hair color had been before the sun bleached it—and imagining how they'd look in makeup.

A man in a business suit strolled up to the surfer girls' table. He had a smooth grin and carried himself like a movie star.

"Hey, mind if I sit?" he asked, nodding to an empty chair.

A girl in a pink bikini looked up. "Uh, sure?" she said, obviously not wanting to be rude.

He plopped down. "Surfers?"

They nodded cautiously.

"I surf every morning, when I travel." He let out a small laugh. "One time, I wiped out so hard in Bali, I thought I'd lost my board forever. It washed up two miles down the coast, and by the time I got there, a local kid had painted it with these wild designs. Looked way better than when I first bought it."

As the girls laughed he continued with his story. "The waves were crazy that day, and I was pretty sure I was gonna get wiped out again, but I managed to pull it together just before I got sucked under. Best feeling ever."

Mei leaned toward Max. "I feel bad for listening, but the guy's a good storyteller," she whispered.

"Yeah," Max agreed quietly, sipping his smoothie. "I *think* he might be trying to pick them up?"

Mei snorted. "No way. He's like, a hundred years older than them!"

Then the guy pulled two gold tickets from his pocket. "Check it out. VIP passes to Starlight Riot."

Max sat up straight. "Holy crap! I absolutely love those guys!" he whispered.

Mei nodded; her own eyes were wide. She'd tried desperately to get tickets but the concert had sold out in minutes.

The man leaned in a little too close to the girl in the pink bikini, lowering his voice, "Wanna go? Just you and me?"

The surfer girl's smile froze, her gaze flicking nervously to her friends. "Uh, thanks, but I think we're good."

"Oh, come on," the man pressed. His demeanor changed, and suddenly he didn't look quite so nice. He looked... pushy. "Just you and me, babe."

Max glanced to Mei, sharing a look—the dude was a creep.

Luckily, it seemed like the girl in the pink bikini was having the same thoughts. She shook her head. "No thanks," she said again, more firmly. "I'll be out of town. Surfing trip."

Instead of taking the hint, the man turned to the next girl at the table. "How 'bout you, beautiful?"

When she said no, he moved on to the next one. The girls were looking more and more uncomfortable, and eventually, Max had

had enough. His chair scraped as he stood. "Can't you tell when you're not wanted?"

The man looked over his shoulder. "This doesn't concern you. Keep out of it," he sneered.

Mei rose to her feet beside Max. "Pretty sure this doesn't concern you either." She pulled out her phone. "And with that in mind, I'm calling the cops."

The man turned as other teens in the restaurant began to gang up on him. "Whatever," he muttered. With a snort, he threw the tickets on the floor. "I wouldn't want to see these guys anyway."

He stormed from the restaurant.

The surfer girls sighed in relief as Max and Mei sat back down. Mei gave a nervous laugh, her heart pounding. "I can't believe I... did we just do that?"

Max bit his lip. "That was crazy. I thought I was about to get punched!"

They were interrupted by the girl in the pink bikini. "Thank you so much," she gushed, approaching their table.

"Don't think about it. The dude was a creep."

"I'm Kaia," she said, also introducing her friends, Lani and Piper. Max and Mei chatted for a while, with Kaia explaining how she came to the beach most mornings to surf. When Max and Mei mentioned they were YouTubers, her eyes lit up.

"Whoa, that's awesome! I'm just getting into makeup myself, so I could definitely use some tips. And I suck at video games, so,

Max, you'd better make sure your videos work for console players, too."

Max laughed. "I'll keep that in mind." But then he grew more serious. "I'm sorry that guy bothered you. You should never have to put up with creeps like that."

Kaia sighed. "He was better than most. At least he told a good story." She forced a laugh. "Almost thought he was genuine there for a minute!"

Mei nodded. "He def started strong. The story about Bali? It hooked us, too!"

"Yeah," Max agreed, "but then he showed his true colors. A good story doesn't matter if the person telling it isn't genuine."

Mei nodded slowly, her eyes narrowing in thought. "You're right. It's like YouTube. You can use storytelling to pull people in, but if you're not genuine, they'll figure it out, and you'll lose them."

Max grinned. "For sure. Storytelling for the power of good, not creepy evil."

Kaia laughed. "I love it! Do me a favor though, if you're going to use it for the power of good, get to the good stuff fast. I once had this guy take twenty minutes to introduce himself!"

"What was his name?"

Kaia cringed. "No idea. I excused myself before he got to it!"

Mei snorted, almost causing smoothie to exit from her nose. "Okay, got it. Short intros. Get to the good stuff fast! Don't be a creep."

They all laughed.

"Hey, I don't suppose either of you like Starlight Riot?" Kaia asked. She pulled out the left-behind tickets. "I'd kill to go, but not at the risk of meeting that creep again." She grimaced. "It'd be just like him to wait by the front gate."

Max and Mei exchanged a glance. "We're both huge fans!"

When Kaia was back at her table, Max raised his smoothie in a toast. "To storytelling that doesn't make people run for the door."

Mei clinked her cup against his, smiling. "And free tickets to Starlight Riot!"

11
DON'T BE LIKE CREEPY GUY!

Know your target audience

Max and Mei had just finished a refreshing swim in the ocean. They toweled off, laughing about their attempts to catch the perfect wave. After a quick change, they settled back at their favorite spot in their beach café, ready to work on their YouTube channels.

There were actually several cafes at the beach, all in a row. Each had its own vibe—reggae beats at one, sleek lattes and fancy cars at another. Naturally, Max and Mei had picked the liveliest spot, where kids their age hung out and music blasted from the speakers.

The surfer girls were just leaving as they arrived, waving brightly to their heroes as they passed, again promising to subscribe to Max and Mei's new channels. Mei shook her head, remembering how they'd met. "That guy was a total creep," she said. "And even if he wasn't, he was way too old."

Her forehead wrinkled. "Pretty sure the whole 'surfer' thing was a lie, too."

Max laughed. "Yeah, it was cringe. He just didn't get they weren't interested."

"It's a perfect example of why knowing your audience is so important. I mean, he did some basic research—he knew about Starlight Riot—but if you don't connect genuinely, people will see right through you."

Max leaned back in his chair, sipping his smoothie. "So, how do we make sure we're not *that guy* in our videos?"

Mei gazed down the row of beachfront cafés. She tapped her teeth in thought. "Ever notice how each of these places is totally different?" she asked eventually.

Max followed her gaze, giving the question some thought. "Like that one over there blasting reggae music?" Max asked. "Or the super fancy one?" He pulled face. "Neither are really my scene."

"Exactly!" Mei enthused. "Each café knows who they're for. *And* they follow through on what their look promises, once you're inside. The reggae place has chillout hammocks. And I can see at least five people sipping espressos at the nicer place."

Max frowned. "So, the lesson here is about being... what's that word... where you're true to yourself?"

"Authentic?"

"Yeah, authentic!" he said. "You're saying it's no good drawing people in with false promises. We have to carry through! If we're authentic and actually give our audience what they care about, they'll stick with us."

"Right," Mei nodded, flipping back through her notes. "And that means we've got to pay attention to what they respond to—look at the comments, see which videos get the most views, and figure out why. That's where creepy dude fell down. He wasn't reading the room."

Max took a huge slurp of smoothie, leaning back. "Who would have thought hanging out at a café could teach us so much?"

Mei leaned back in her own chair with a sigh. "I know, right? We should do it more often!"

12
TACO 'BOUT UNIQUE STYLE

Developing unique style and personality

The next day, Max and Mei met up at their favorite beachside food truck, Taco Hang Ten. Painted in bright turquoise and orange, with murals of waves and surfers splashed across the sides, the truck was hard to miss. Lively music pumped from speakers, and the staff handed out tacos with wide smiles and jokes that seemed to make every customer a little happier.

When their tacos arrived, Max and Mei found a spot under a nearby palm tree and dug in. As Max took a bite, he looked around, noticing the whole vibe of the place—the bold colors, the beachy decor, the fun banter from the staff. "This truck just gets it," he said with a grin. "I mean, it totally stands out, you know? The colors, the murals, the whole vibe. It's, like, *fun* and memorable."

Mei nodded around her own mouthful. "It's the kind of place you remember and want to come back to," she agreed. Glancing around at the bustling scene, she said, "I think we need something like that in our videos. We're putting out good content, but it could be... I don't know, more *us*?"

They continued to eat in silence, until Max suddenly pulled out his phone. Holding his taco between his teeth, he began typing.

"What?" he asked when Mei snorted.

"Writing things down? I must be rubbing off on you."

He bit defensively into his taco. "I had an idea, okay?"

Mei raised an eyebrow, reaching for the phone. "Spill."

He jerked it away. "It's probably stupid."

Mei laughed, making another play for his phone. "You're not getting out of it that easily. Spill!"

Max sighed. "Well," he said nervously. "I'm thinking, what if kicked things up a little? You know, a funny intro, maybe something that grabs people from the first second. It couldn't hurt, right? A clip of me messing up a jump, then straight into a play-by-play on how to nail it next time."

"I like it!"

"You do?" he asked, surprised.

"Yeah. It suits your vibe—*helpful and entertaining*."

Max sat back. "I like that! Helpful and entertaining!"

When Mei continued to look at him expectantly, he frowned. "What?"

When she looked very pointedly at his phone, his eyes widened. "Okay, okay! I'm writing it down!"

Mei laughed.

Inspired, Mei began sketching in her own book.

Like the food truck, a unique style would reflect who she was and make her stand out. It would also help draw in the *right* sort of customers. No point advertising tacos if all you sold was spaghetti.

"So what's my unique style?" she muttered. "Bold lines? Simple shades?" She began drawing sketches for different makeup designs, before slapping her forehead. "I'm thinking too physical! It's not about the content! It's about how I present it! Should I be funny? Serious? Geeky… ooh, I like geeky. I could totally do that!" She got back to work, muttering all the while.

Beside her, Max was lost in his own eureka moment, typing madly on his phone. Seating was limited around the taco van, and several times a stranger approached to share their bench. They'd stop as they approached, noting the muttering and crazy, excited looks, then back very slowly away.

Max and Mei didn't notice. They were having too much fun.

13
SIGNS, STRINGS, AND FIRST IMPRESSIONS

Hooking viewers and creating quality content

Max and Mei had just finished their tacos. They were strolling along the beach promenade and the sun was beginning to set, casting a golden hue over the pavers, grass, sand, and waves. They soon passed the café where they'd brainstormed the previous day, the tables now filled with people laughing and clinking glasses as string lights flickered on overhead.

They lingered nearby, watching as people drifted in and out of cafés, some pausing at the sign out front to scan the menu, others peeking inside before choosing another place down the row.

Max tilted his head, studying the crowd. "Looks like the folks who stop at the sign are deciding pretty quick."

Mei nodded as she swigged the last of her soda. "Yeah, it's like they know right away if it's what they want. Some of them barely read two lines."

Max's brow furrowed as he watched a couple glance at the sign, then head in without a second thought. "Guess it's all about grabbing attention right from the start? Either it clicks, or… well, they move on."

They continued walking, the sounds of laughter and clinking glasses drifting from the café behind them.

After a pause, Mei glanced sideways at Max. "I think that's kind of like our videos. First few seconds are the sign. People either get pulled in or they're gone."

A street performer set up on the corner, plugging an electric guitar into an amp. Tuning her strings, she unleashed an electrifying riff that caused Max and Mei to immediately stop and watch. Beside them, others did the same.

When she finished, the musician looked up, introduced herself, and then launched into her first song.

"Huh," muttered Mei.

"What?"

"You know what we were just talking about? The first few seconds? I think she just did that here."

"But she was just warming up!"

"Uh huh. And she did it in a way that made us stop. Think we'd still be here if she spent half an hour plucking each string individually?"

"Oh."

Mei grinned. "Yeah. She's good. She made sure we knew it, too."

Max pulled out his phone, scrolling through some of his videos as the musician launched into another ripper of a tune. "Makes me think," he said. "Sometimes I get all caught up in talking, explaining every little detail. Maybe I should just get right into it, hook them with something interesting right off the bat. Like she did."

"Exactly!" Mei said, watching as the musician pulled off a series of impressive riffs to cheers and applause. They found a patch of grass and settled in for a free show. "I guess, the best stuff grabs you from the first note!"

14
IT'S A TWO-WAY STREET

Engaging with the audience

Max and Mei settled into the back seat of the taxi, the hum of the engine and the gentle sway of the vehicle a calming end to their busy day. The sky outside was painted in hues of orange and pink as the sun set over the ocean. Max pulled out his phone, aimlessly scrolling through his social media feeds, while Mei did the same beside him.

"Hey, check this out," Max said, nudging Mei with his elbow. He turned his phone towards her, displaying the food truck's Instagram page. "The food truck from earlier is blowing up online."

Mei leaned in, intrigued. The food truck's account was filled with vibrant photos of their dishes, but what caught her attention was the comment section. "Look at this," she said, pointing to a post with hundreds of comments. "They're responding to almost every comment. And not just generic replies—personalized responses."

Max scrolled down further. "And they're running polls on what new taco flavor to introduce next. They're even letting whoever invents the winning flavor name it. Genius!"

Mei's eyes sparkled as she scrolled through the comments. She noticed a picture of a customer holding a taco named after them, grinning from ear to ear. Meanwhile, Max watched a short video clip where the food truck owner thanked a fan who'd suggested a new salsa recipe.

Max's scrolling was interrupted by a YouTube notification.

RaynCloud123: Great video! Any chance you can do a walkthrough on level 3?

Someone had commented on one of his videos! A tingle traveled down his spine. He only had a 150 subscribers so far (151 if you counted his mom), and he thought Mei had similar. It was such a buzz when someone took the time to comment!

He tapped the notification bubble, typing a quick reply.

Maxinator: thx man!! ooof lvl 3 is brutal ;p def can do a walkthrough 4 U stay tuned!

As he hit send, he caught Mei's amused smile from the corner of his eye. "What?" he asked, feeling defensive.

"Nothing," she laughed. "It's just... I think you might've just done your first 'personalized response.'"

Max laughed too, realizing she was right. "Guess I did. Feels pretty good, actually."

They lapsed into silence as the taxi continued on, Mei's fingers drumming a rhythm on her notebook. Finally, she looked up, eyes bright. "You know what could be fun? Asking our followers what they want to see next—see what they're into."

"Think they'd answer? Kinda feels like making them do the work for us."

She looked at him flatly. "Max, you just had RaynCloud123 email you out of the blue to make a request. I'm starting to think our viewers might *want* to be part of the action.

The taxi hit a bump, jostling them slightly. Max scratched his head. "I guess maybe it's like a two-way thing? The more we reach out, the more they reach back… and we get, like, a vibe on what's working."

"Exactly," Mei replied. "Also, I don't know about you, but if a YouTuber I like ever replies back to me, I'm a superfan for life."

Max chuckled. "Yeah. Guilty as well."

Mei flipped open her notebook. "I should do a poll tomorrow. Ask who I should cosplay for my next look." She shot Max a glance. "And no, you're not allowed to vote for Batman."

Max feigned disappointment. "Fine. But only if you promise to actually post the look they pick." He looked again at the message from RaynCloud123. "Let's start tonight. I'll post a poll asking which game I should cover next, and you can ask for character suggestions for your next transformation."

"Deal," Mei agreed, offering a fist bump.

The taxi pulled up to Mei's house, and they parted with a surge of excitement. Yes, they only had a hundred or so subscribers. But a little voice was whispering at the back of their minds that if they did this properly—create videos with a unique style, hit viewers hard in the first few seconds with something interesting, and then engage with their audience after, those numbers wouldn't stay so low for long.

15
REVISE AND SHINE

Review and improve

Several days had passed since Max and Mei decided to get more interactive with their audience. They met up at the beach café, their usual hangout, the salty breeze mixing with the aroma of fresh pastries. The place was buzzing, much like their own excitement.

Max pulled out his laptop, face lighting up as he logged into his YouTube account. "Alright, let's see what we've got. My poll on which game to cover next blew up!" He scrolled through the results, eyes wide. "Looks like everyone's itching for me to dive into *Breath of the Wild*. This is gonna be epic."

Mei sipped her mango smoothie, her eyes sparkling over the rim of the glass. "That's awesome! My viewers had a lot to say, too." She opened her phone, scrolling through comments. "Kaia and her friends—you remember the surfer girls?—tried out my makeup techniques, but they said it didn't work well on tanned skin. They're wondering if I can suggest alternative products."

"Sounds like a new video idea," Max said, nudging her playfully.

"Totally. I want everyone to feel included." She held up a finger. "Oh, and get this—they loved the backstory of the character I featured. They're asking for more behind-the-scenes stuff, not just the tutorials."

Max grinned. "Looks like we're both leveling up. Check this out." He turned his laptop toward her, showcasing a folder bursting with fan art. "I asked for submissions, and some of these are next-level amazing."

Mei leaned in closer, jaw dropping. "Whoa! That Master Sword illustration is insane. You should totally feature it."

"Planning on it. Thinking of putting it up in the background of my next video." He ran a hand through his hair, shaking his head in disbelief. "It's wild seeing how talented everyone is."

"It's kind of surreal, isn't it?" Mei mused. "People actually engaging with what we're putting out there."

Max nodded, his gaze drifting toward the ocean. "Makes all the late nights worth it."

Mei chuckled, then let out a dramatic sigh. "Speaking of late nights, I had no idea doing things properly would take so much time. Editing my videos, adjusting sound levels, adding text—it takes me three times longer than just filming!"

"Preach," Max laughed. "Editing is a beast."

"But the final product?" Her eyes lit up. "So worth it. My videos actually look professional now, not like some kid messing around with a camera." She giggled. "Even if that's exactly what I am."

"You're a pro in disguise," Max winked.

"I'm thinking maybe I can make the process easier," she said, sitting straighter. "If I set up in a quiet spot, I won't have to edit out random noises. And good lighting means less tweaking later."

"Work smarter, not harder," Max agreed. "I started doing that with my game recordings. Saves a ton of time."

Mei glanced back at her phone. "Oh! I was also thinking of doing a live Q&A during a makeup session. You know, answer questions on the fly."

"That would be awesome," Max said. "I might steal that idea and do a live stream while gaming."

"See? We're full of brilliant ideas today," Mei laughed.

They spent the next hour bouncing concepts off each other, scribbling notes on napkins, their excitement building with each new thought. The café buzzed around them, but they were lost in their own creative world.

As the sun began to dip, casting a golden hue over everything, Max stretched his arms, a satisfied smile on his face.. "I feel like we're onto something big."

"Me too," Mei agreed. She gazed at the horizon, the sky painted in shades of pink and orange. "It's like our channels are becoming more than just videos—they're turning into communities."

"Exactly," Max said, his eyes meeting hers. "And it's all because we're connecting with people, not just talking at them."

Mei smiled, feeling a warm glow of satisfaction. "Who knew that listening could make such a difference?"

They packed up their things, still chatting animatedly.

"On a different topic, I was looking at my old videos the other day," Max said as he slung his backpack over one shoulder, "I think I need to have my mic slightly further from my mouth. I get this distortion when I yell."

Mei snorted. "For someone that's supposed to know a level inside out, you get jump scared *a lot.*"

"Hey! It's procedurally generated!"

"Still hilarious. But yeah, good pickup. See you next Saturday?"

Next Saturday was the Starlight Riot concert. They still couldn't believe they'd managed to score tickets.

"Wouldn't miss it. Think we can make 500 subscribers before then?"

Mei laughed. "Heck yeah, let's do this!"

As they parted ways, Mei felt a surge of motivation. Once home, she set up her filming area as she'd promised—good lighting, a quiet corner, everything within reach. Maybe this would make editing less of a marathon.

She hit record, diving into a new tutorial that included product options for different skin types, inspired by Kaia and her friends. As she worked, she found herself just really... *enjoying* the process. She could picture her viewers following along. This was the sort of thing she'd do just for fun, even if she couldn't ever make an income.

Meanwhile, Max was at his own desk, setting up a live stream event and pinning up the fan art he'd received. The room felt different now—more like a shared space between him and his audience. Shortly before going live, he also adjusted his microphone just ever slightly backward. Lucky thing too—his first jump scare was only five minutes in.

Both of them were embracing the journey, not just the destination. By involving their viewers, reviewing and consciously improving, they weren't just creating content; they were refining their craft.

MEI'S NOTES:
CREATING COMPELLING CONTENT

Brainstorm and plan ahead
Effective content creation starts with dedicated brainstorming and planning sessions, leading to better videos and smoother production.

Incorporate storytelling
Weave storytelling elements into content to keep it engaging. Share interesting backstories, character narratives, or personal anecdotes to make videos more relatable and captivating.

Know your audience
Genuine connection with the audience is crucial; insincerity is easily spotted and can drive viewers away, as demonstrated by that creep who misread the room.

Develop a unique style
Establishing a distinct style and personality helps stand out, just like the taco truck's memorable vibe attracted customers; embracing one's uniqueness draws the right audience.

Hook viewers immediately

Capturing attention in the first few seconds is essential, like how the street performer's electrifying riff made everyone stop and watch.

Engage with the audience

Actively interacting with viewers through comments, polls, and personalized responses builds a stronger connection and fosters community.

Review and improve

Continuously reviewing content helps identify areas for improvement, such as fixing lighting issues in future videos to enhance quality.

Work smarter, not harder

Setting up the filming environment properly - with good lighting and minimal noise - saves time in editing and results in better videos.

Doing things properly takes time

Investing additional time in editing and adding finishing touches significantly enhances the overall quality of the content.

Build a community

Being interactive and genuine can transform a channel into a growing community, strengthening viewer loyalty and engagement.

Note to self

Don't laugh while sipping smoothie; it almost came out my nose!

PART 4: BUILDING YOUR BRAND

In which our intrepid heroes discover that forging a brand runs deeper than logos and lighting—it means shaping a style that's instantly recognizable—and learn that even a false start can lead to backstage revelations.

16
GETTING READY FOR THE CONCERT

Understanding your brand

Max and Mei were in Mei's room, getting ready for the concert. Posters of Starlight Riot had been taped to the wall and a string of fairy lights cast a warm glow around the room. Mei was rifling through her closet, tossing clothes onto her bed, while Max lounged on a beanbag, scrolling through his phone.

"I can't believe we're seeing Starlight Riot live!" Mei exclaimed, pulling out a glittery top. "Imagine if we actually met them!"

Max snorted. "We'll be in the crowd, not some VIP in the wings." He bit his lip. "Would be awesome though."

"You never know," said Mei, unperturbed. She held the top against herself in the mirror. "What are you wearing?"

Max grinned. "Something cool, obviously. But hey, while we're getting ready, I was thinking we should vlog about the concert."

Mei paused, holding a pair of jeans. "Thoughts?"

Max cocked his head. "Needs more rips."

"My thoughts exactly." She got to work with a pair of scissors, teasing out the threads. "Regarding the vlog stuff, just filming the concert doesn't feel very 'on brand' for me. Like, I'm not a music channel, I'm a makeup channel, you know?"

Max nodded. "Fair point." They'd hit their targets only last night, racking up over half a thousand subscribers each, although their watch hours—how long people had watched their videos for in total—was still low at twenty-five. And while they wanted to keep the momentum going, Mei had a point. Still... "How about filming yourself getting ready? You could do your makeup, talk about the concert and then have a clip of it all streaky and worn at the end of Starlight. Would that suit your channel?"

Mei grinned evilly. "How about I do concert makeup for *you*?"

"No way."

"Pleeeease?" Mei asked, batting her eyelashes. "It would tie in soooo well with my makeup channel."

Max hesitated. "Makeup? Isn't that just for girls?"

Mei smiled, attempting to reassure him. "Heaps of guys wear makeup nowadays! Remember Jake, from the electronics store?"

"No way."

"Way."

"I thought he just had really good eyes," muttered Max.

"Nope. Eyeliner." She fluttered her eyes again. "Pleeeease? It'll be super subtle, *and* it'll show our viewers a different side of us."

Max sighed, still uncertain. "Alright, but only if it's subtle. And manly. And you *have* to make me look good."

Mei laughed, grabbing her makeup bag. "Deal!."

As Mei began applying the makeup, she explained each step to camera, her voice calming and professional. "I'm just going to add a bit of foundation to even out your skin tone. And a little eyeliner to make your eyes pop, but nothing too crazy."

Max closed his eyes, feeling the soft brush against his skin. "You really know what you're doing, huh?"

Mei smiled, concentrating. "Yep, it's my thing. Just like you're amazing at explaining game strategies, I'm great at this."

When she finished, Max looked in the mirror. His eyes widened at what he saw. "Wow, I actually look... great. This is awesome!"

Mei beamed. "Told you! Now we're both ready to rock this concert. And it ties into my makeup brand perfectly."

Max nodded, his excitement growing. "You're right. I'm still struggling to think about how Starlight can tie into mine. Maybe I could relate the band to game characters or something?"

Mei laughed. "Don't push it. Remember the creepy café dude?"

"How could I forget? He gave us our tickets!"

"Well, don't be like creepy dude. Don't force things."

"You're right," Max said with a nod. He reached for a makeup brush. "Now, since you did my makeup, it's only fair I do yours."

Mei screamed in mock horror. "*On brand*, Max. We need to stay *on brand*! And mine is definitely not *laughing stock*."

17
FAKES AND LADDERS

The importance of a good logo

When Max and Mei stepped off the bus for the concert, they were hit by an electricity in the air that dialed their excitement from ten out of ten, to eleven. The air buzzed with anticipation, and the scent of food trucks and fresh grass mingled together. The open-air concert was at a local stadium outside town. Set in the middle of lush parklands, the scent of grass and blooming flowers mingled with the distant thrum of the stadium's warm-up band. Crowds dressed in vibrant outfits and band merch swarmed the pathways, their energy infectious.

As they walked toward the stadium, Max noticed a group of girls strolling by, their eyes briefly meeting his. One of them flashed a shy smile and whispered to her friend, who giggled and glanced back at him. Max felt a warm flush creep up his cheeks.

Mei elbowed him gently. "See? Told you those dreamy eyes would get attention."

Max chuckled, feeling a mix of embarrassment and newfound

confidence as the excitement of the night built around them. When they approached the entrance, they could hear the excited chatter of fans and occasional cheers from inside.

Unfortunately, that's where things all went wrong. When the gate attendant scanned their tickets, her device flashed red. The attendant frowned, scanning the tickets again. "These tickets are fake," she said, handing them back.

Max's face turned bright red. "What? That's impossible! We got them from-"

Mei grabbed Max's arm, dragging him away. She'd been examining her ticket, and her eyes had gone wide with realization. "Max, wait. Look at the logo on these tickets." She held them against a poster nearby. "See? The colors are off. And the star is different!"

Max held up his own ticket, noticing the dull, mismatched colors and off-center star, and his excitement deflated like a punctured balloon. "Crap on a stick!" he swore. The logo on the poster was bright, the colors popped and everything aligned perfectly. The logo on theirs did not.

His voice was pleading. "What do we do?"

Mei slumped, her shoulders sagging. "What can we do? We go home, I guess."

Max swore some more, but eventually, they decided to leave. "Let's get out of here before the crowd gets worse," he muttered. He eyed the packed throngs of people. "We can take the bus from the other side of the park, where it's less crowded."

"Do you know where to go?"

"Yeah," Max muttered. He pointed to a water tower looking over the stadium. "It's about ten minutes past that."

The muffled roar of the crowd seemed to mock Max and Mei as they skirted the stadium walls. They walked in silence; each dimly heard guitar riff a stab through their intestines. Lost in their thoughts, their earlier excitement was a dull ache they couldn't wait to escape by bus.

Max kicked at a rock. "I was really looking forward to this," he muttered.

"I know."

"That douchebag at the café wasn't ever going to bring Kaia here. I bet he had a whole pocket full of fake printouts! No wonder he couldn't be bothered picking them up."

They'd just passed the stadium, climbing a low rise to the water tower, when they heard the crowd go ballistic behind them. Even through the stadium's thick walls they heard people hollering and screaming. Starlight Riot had taken the stage.

Max stopped, his face contorting. "We're missing it, Mei. We're really missing it."

Mei placed a hand on his shoulder. "Unless you can fly, there's not much we can do about it. Those stadium walls have got to be twenty feet high, at least!"

Max didn't respond, his eyes looking up. After several seconds, he said, "Mei, how high do you think this water tower is?"

She shrugged. "Maybe forty feet? Why.... *Oh.*"

"Are you thinking what I'm thinking?"

Mei's eyes sparkled with anticipation. "Let's do it."

In excitement, they scaled the old water tower, the metal ladder creaking beneath their weight. It was taller than they'd thought, and with the added height of the rise it stood upon, gave panoramic views of the stadium.

Max whistled, sitting to dangle his feet from the edge. "Oh man, this is so cool." They were directly behind the stage, so couldn't see the band in person, but had a stellar view of one of the huge LED screens ringing the stadium. And more importantly, crystal clear music echoed up to meet them.

Mei joined him, nodding. "You could always tell it was Starlight Riot—they have this... *feel* that shines through everything they do—but I must say it's nice to hear them clearly."

Max leaned back, taking in the view. "*Feel.* I like that word. Like a sound signature."

Mei nudged the fake tickets still in his pocket. "Not just sound."

Max pulled the tickets out, comparing the logo to the massive billboards before them. "Yeah, you're right. As soon as you look closely, it's obvious they're fake."

His nose scrunched up. "Think we'll be like that one day?"

When she glanced at him, he explained. "So big that people try to make fake tickets to attend our live streams."

"I hope so." She pulled out her sketch book and started drawing. "Though, we'd need logos, first, for someone to fake them."

He looked over her shoulder. "What are you doing?"

"Designing logos, of course. Yours should have something to do with games, I think. Maybe a stylized controller?" She bit her lip, moving onto another design. "Needs to be memorable… recognizable. Like a signature that someone can use to find your page."

She flipped her book around. "What do you think? Any of these work?"

Max whistled in appreciation. In the space of a minute she'd sketched five different designs across the page. He took the book, examining each in turn.

Finally, he pointed at design four, which was a stylized controller with the words 'PRESS START' emblazoned across it. "This one, I think. It's instantly recognizable, unique, and tells people exactly what I'm here to do." His head cocked. "It would look good as a thumbnail, too."

He looked up at her. "Thanks."

Their favorite song came on, and they both started singing.

18
BRAND NEW HEIGHTS

Brand identity

Sometime later, Max leaned back, the sound of the roaring crowd filling his ears. "This view is amazing. You can *feel* the energy." He chuckled. "I'm almost happy we didn't get let in. *Almost*."

Mei nodded. The lights from the stage lit up the night, but even without them, she'd have known who was playing. "Their style, their sound... everything is so distinctly Starlight Riot."

His grin turned sheepish. "Yeah. One proper look at those tickets and we should have known something was off. It just didn't have the same... look, as everything else. Like, Starlight Riot tickets would have been brighter, and on better paper. And the star in the logo wasn't centered, like it is literally *everywhere* else."

Mei kicked her legs gently. "Don't beat yourself up. I missed it too. But yeah, that's what makes their brand so strong. It's not just the logo either, it's like their brand identity is *bright*, *bold* and *quality*. Everything our tickets were not."

When Max didn't answer, Mei looked over. "Hey, I missed it too. Don't stress! Best seats in the house up here!"

Max chuckled. "Nah, that's not what got me."

"Then what?"

Again, that sheepish look crossed his eyes. He scratched the back of his head. "Ahh… What does *Brand Identity* mean?"

"You don't know?"

His shoulders hunched. "I'm not smart like you," he muttered.

Mei chuckled. "You're plenty smart. I wasn't making fun of you. Just, sometimes I use big words for simple things. Brand Identity is like a person's personality, but for a brand. Like, how you can tell a Starlight Riot song from just a few notes, or how their logo and colors are instantly recognizable."

She gestured toward the strobe lights below. "Brand Identity is your signature look. We're going to want it for our channels, too, I guess. It's that look and feel on your thumbnail, for example, that makes people instantly know it's your video."

Max grinned, punching her arm. "Why didn't you say so, then?"

Mei leaned back, her eyes drifting back to the stage, though he could tell her focus was beyond it. "We're going to make our channels shine, just like Starlight Riot. It's all about creating a brand that's unmistakably us."

Max laughed, the sound blending with the music below. "Consistent and memorable, right?"

Mei grinned. "Exactly." She looked at him sideways. "Also, if you call me a nerd for knowing what Brand Identity is, I'm throwing you off this ledge."

19
CONSISTENCY IS KEY(CARD)

Be consistent with branding

Starlight Riot were taking a drink break when a beam of light cut through the darkness below.

"Hey, who's up there?" called a gruff voice. A flashlight swept over the tower.

Max and Mei exchanged wide-eyed looks. Mei grabbed Max's arm, and they scurried back from the edge just moments before the beam passed. They crouched low, hearts pounding.

"I don't think he saw us," Max whispered, grinning despite the situation. "This is so cool. Like I'm in a real-life stealth game. Where's a cardboard box when you need one?"

Mei didn't look quite so thrilled. "What if we get caught! I don't want to go to jail!" She fumbled in her pocket for her phone.

"Good thinking," whispered Max. "This will make a great vlog!"

But Mei didn't open her camera. Instead, she opened YouTube. As the security guard's footsteps got closer, Max watched, intrigued, as Mei entered the keywords 'two cats fighting.'

She hit play just as the crunch of gravel on boots stopped below them. Yowling and hissing filled the air, echoing through the silent night.

The guard paused, the flashlight beam lingering. "Just cats," he muttered. His footsteps retreated, the light fading away as the band started their next song.

Max and Mei let out twin breaths as their heartbeats returned to normal. Max collapsed backward, his arms spread wide. "That was close," he said to the stars. "Nice save with the cat video."

Mei smiled. "Thanks," she replied, putting her phone away. They were both still whispering. "Let's keep a low profile for a few minutes, just in case the guard returns."

Max nodded, and they both crept to the edge. He spotted the guard, who was now walking back to the stadium. "What made you think of cat videos? That was genius!"

Mei shrugged. "It's like those fake tickets. As soon as we looked closely, we knew something was off. I figured here, we wanted the opposite. The guard had to hear something consistent with what he'd expect to make a loud noise. I came up with cats."

"Genius," Max reiterated.

His comment made Mei blush. "Not really. I just thought we needed something that fit perfectly with the situation."

Max leaned back, staring up at the sky. "Yeah, it totally worked. It's like when you're playing a game and something feels out of place—it's not even a concious thing. You notice right away..."

They sat in silence for several seconds, listening to the music wash over the park. *Midnight Run* was a fan favorite, though they'd had reservations when the band first announced it.

Running wild through city lights,
Chasing dreams and neon nights,
Every corner holds a new surprise,
Under the stars, see us rise.

Suddenly, Max sat up straight. "Hey, you don't think we should be doing that with our videos, do you?"

Mei's face screwed up. "What, running wild through the city?"

Max rolled his eyes. "No, that thing you were talking about before. Consistency."

"What do you mean?"

He leaned forward. "Like, everything we put out needs to fit together perfectly. The cat video convinced the guard because it fit what he expected. If our videos, thumbnails, and posts all match, people will trust us and know what to expect. Consistent brand identity."

Mei laughed. "Now who's the nerd?" But she quickly held up her hands. "Just joking. You're totally right. That's what makes Starlight Riot so memorable, when you think about it. Their brand is strong and consistent in everything they do."

"It will help viewers trust us, too," Max added. "Remember when they first announced *Midnight Run*? I had no idea how they'd make a song about jogging work, but I trusted them. Everything they do reflects who they are—the band, the brand, the sound. When we announce a new video, our past consistency will help our viewers trust that they'll like it just as much as the old stuff!"

"You're right," Mei breathed. "It's about more than just having a cool logo or catchphrase. It's about the intro and outro, the thumbnails, the on-screen graphics, how we structure our videos and how long they are. Even our tone of voice and energy!"

"Hey, it's *also* about a good catchphrase," Max drawled. The security guard had reached the stadium now, entering via a side door that he opened with a keycard. Not needing to be quiet anymore, Max stood up. "My catchphrase is going to be, *welcome to awesome town!*"

Mei laughed, covering her mouth to muffle the sound. "A catchphrase is great branding. A lame one is not."

Max chuckled. "Point taken. I'll work on it," he said, sitting back down. His movements stopped though, leaving him in a half crouch. His eyes narrowed, focused on the door the security guard had just walked through. "Mei," he hissed.

She stilled as he gestured her over, looking nervously around. "Another guard?"

Max shook his head. A huge grin slid across his face. But

instead of answering, he pointed.

"Oh," Mei said. Then she said it again, louder. "*Oh!*"

Together they scrambled for the ladder, racing from it toward the stadium… and a very particular side door, which a security guard had forgotten to close behind them.

20
KEEPING IT REAL

Be genuine

Max and Mei crept through the open door. On the other side was a dimly lit hallway. Exposed pipes ran along the ceiling, faded posters lined the walls and the distant sound of a crowd shouting "*Encore! Encore!*" echoed toward them. They looked at each other; eyes wide.

"Backstage," Max whispered. Mei just nodded, not trusting herself to speak. Grabbing lanyards with the letters VIP stamped across them from a peg by the door, they crept forward. The hallway stretched endlessly; every turn was a spike of fear that they'd find Security waiting for them on the other side.

A door rattled on their left. Mei and Max froze as a stagehand stepped out, adjusting her headset. She stopped when she saw them. "Who are you?" she asked.

Max and Mei both answered at the same time.

"Backup dancers."

"Street team."

There was a moment of awkward silence before Max coughed. "Just joking. About being a backup dancer. I'm totally, ah, on the street team too."

The stagehand chuckled. "You internet peeps—love your work." Her hand went to her headset. "Gotta run." Then she was off jogging down the corridor.

Mei slumped against the wall. "Backup dancer? Really?"

"I panicked, okay?" Max muttered, slumping against the door the stagehand had come through. "It was all I could think.... whoah!" The door swung inward, and he fell backward with a cry.

Mei rushed lifted from the wall, teasing forgotten. "You okay?" she asked from the doorway?

Max rubbed his backside as he stood. "Guess the door didn't lock," he said sheepishly. He stepped back outside. "Come on—set's almost over. Let's find the wings, see Starlight before they go offstage."

But Mei didn't move, even when he tugged her. She was staring through the doorway that had just opened. "Max?"

"Yes."

"Pinch me."

Max frowned. "Excuse me?"

"Pinch me. I think I'm dreaming."

"Uh, okay?" he said, reaching forward. But before he could do as requested, she'd darted through the still open door. He followed into a brightly lit room.

Hair styling tools cluttered a shelf in the far corner, beside of sequined outfits and leather jackets. A long makeup mirror ringed with lightbulbs lined one wall, with makeup brushes, eyeshadow palettes, foundation bottles and eyeliner pencils arrayed before it. A table in the corner was laden with snacks and water bottles. A faint smell of hairspray lingered in the air.

"This is... this is..." Mei said, seemingly unable to finish her sentence. "This is..."

"Their dressing room!" Max breathed, finishing her sentence. They'd found Starlight Riot's dressing room!

Mei stepped reverently to the makeup mirror, eyes wide as she surveyed the equipment. Max was halfway to the food table, eager to raid it, when he paused, head cocked. Something was wrong, but he couldn't quite tell what. For the entire time they'd been creeping down the hallway there'd been the heavy thump of bass beneath their feet, and now...

His eyes widened. It was quiet. Too quiet. *The band had stopped playing!*

"We have to go," he hissed. "Show's over! They've left the..."

Words froze in his mouth as the door swung inward, and Starlight Riot walked in, laughing and covered in sweat.

Mei squeaked.

The lead singer paused mid laugh. "Who are you?" he asked, voice suspicious.

Heart pounding in his chest, Max reached for his lanyard.

Should he tell them he was on the Social Team? He glanced to Mei, who had broken out in a cold sweat. What if they got found out? What if the band called the police?

Still... Max swallowed. Something just felt wrong about lying to their idols. Mei, seeming to read his mind, gave a small shake of her head.

His shoulders slumped. "We're... we're huge fans," Max stammered, his voice barely above a whisper. "I'm sorry. We snuck in. We wanted to see you onstage, but accidentally ended up here."

The band members exchanged glances. The lead singer took a step forward, studying them closely. Max's mind raced with thoughts of being kicked out or worse.

But then the lead singer broke into a huge smile. "Well, why didn't you say so?" he laughed. "Fans are why we do this! Come in, take a seat!"

"Really?" Mei asked, eyes wide.

The guitarist raised an eyebrow. "You really shouldn't be back here," he said, softening his words with a smile. "Our security isn't as nice as we are. But I remember trying to sneak backstage at many a concert when I was your age." A hand rubbed through sweat slicked hair. "Never actually managed to do it though. Feel like we should reward someone who did!" she said with a chuckle.

Max and Mei let out a collective sigh. The band members began chatting with them, sharing their excitement and love for music. As they all relaxed, the drummer threw Max a water bottle, instigating a competition to see who could chug theirs the fastest. Neither finished, water spraying across the room as Mei relayed their story about being 'backup dancers.' Turning beet red, Max attempted to wiggle his hips until the lead singer called for him to stop.

"We started out just like you guys," the lead singer reminisced when Max and Mei told the band about their YouTube channels. "Making online music videos, building a brand."

"Any secret sauce you can give us?" Max asked.

The lead singer smiled. "That's easy. Let them see who we really are in your videos. You *can* fake it—a lot of people have an online persona—but it's easier if you're genuine. It's what we did!"

Max scratched his head. "Easy for you to say. You're awesome."

The lead singer snorted. "People connect with people, not content. Trust me—the danger with building a brand is that if you do it wrong, it feels fake. Share personal stories! And behind-the-scenes stuff! It'll make people feel like they're part of the journey."

The bassist coughed. "Just, you know, be careful," she said. "It's a fine line between personal *stories* and personal *information*. Don't ever tell viewers stuff that lets them find you in real-life—your address, school, videos of the front of your house. I learned that the hard way—protect your privacy."

She smiled, leaning back to kick her boots up. "That said, be yourself! Make your viewers feel like they're part of your world. It'll not only feel genuine, it'll be super easy to stay true to brand."

"It's not the only way," the guitarist called from the rear of the room. He hung up his Fender Stratocaster, then joined the conversation. "I mean, look at KISS."

Max pulled a face. "I'm not kissing anyone."

"Nah, the band, man."

"There's a band called KISS?"

"Totally," the guitarist enthused, sticking out his tongue then playing air guitar. "Greatest rock band of all time!"

He caught a bottle of water from the lead singer, then leaned against the makeup table. "They went the total other way—wore mad costumes and makeup out on stage. Had these whole personas. It worked for them because they could be someone else—these crazy characters they couldn't be in real life."

Mei smiled. "Like when I dress up in cosplay."

"Totally! They were like the first cosplayers!"

"So, be genuine, or don't?" Max asked, confused.

The lead singer smiled. "I guess, just be aware there's two different ways you can go. Being genuine is easy if you're even halfway interesting. It's what we did! And what I'd recommend. But some people like the idea of being someone totally different. But not fake!" he said, holding up a finger. "There's a difference. Like with cosplay—you can still tell the people who are really into it, versus the people just doing it because everyone else is."

A well-dressed woman stuck her head into the room. "You okay in here gents?" she asked, interrupting their conversation. Her eyes focused on Max and Mei. "Wed didn't book VIPs tonight." She frowned, stepping into the room. "Who exactly are you?"

The lead singer laughed. "Easy Tabitha. They're with us." He gestured to the woman. "Max and Mei, meet Tabitha." Then he gestured to Max and Mei. "This is our manager, Tabitha."

She shook her head. "I'm sorry, you shouldn't be here. You're going to have to leave."

The band protested, but she shook her head. "No buts. You fly to Europe tomorrow. We do not have time for general chit chat."

"It's okay," Mei said when the band moved to protest. "We should probably get home anyway. This..." she took a deep breath, "has been an absolute blast. Thank you so much for being so nice." She grinned wryly. "And for the YouTube tips." She scribbled Max's and her handles on a page from her notebook, handing it shyly to the band.

The band loaded Max and Mei down with signed posters, guitar picks, and a setlist from the night's performance, insisting that Tabitha send them home in the band's limousine. Max and Mei sat in silence on the plush luxury seats, hearts full and minds buzzing for almost the entirety of the ride.

"That was incredible," Max said eventually, clutching his signed poster.

Mei nodded, her face aglow with excitement. "Max?"

"Yes?"

"Pinch me, please? I want to make sure I'm not dreaming."

MEI'S NOTES:
BUILDING YOUR BRAND

Set clear goals
Always know what you want to achieve with your content, just like we planned to vlog the concert prep experience.

Stay consistent
Your brand should be recognizable and consistent across all platforms. Remember how the fake tickets stood out because the logo wasn't quite right? Consistency builds trust!

Strong brand identity
A unique and memorable brand identity, like Starlight Riot's, helps you stand out. It's not just the logo but the entire vibe.

Engage with your audience
Connect with viewers genuinely, just like Starlight Riot connects with their fans. Engaging with an audience helps build loyalty and boosts visibility.

Thank you, cat videos
Always have a backup plan. You never know when you'll need a cat video to get out of a sticky situation!

Learn from the pros
Take inspiration from those who have made it. Hearing how Starlight Riot started gave us great ideas for our channels.

Have fun
Remember, the journey is as important as the destination. Enjoy every moment, even the unexpected ones, and let that joy shine through in your content.

Be genuine. Or don't!
It's easy to build a brand around being yourself because you don't have to change anything. But plenty of people go the other way too - building an online persona so that their private lives stay separate from their public ones. We need to think about what's going to work for us.

PART 5: ENGAGING WITH YOUR AUDIENCE

In which our intrepid heroes learn that building a loyal audience isn't just about posting content—it's about forging real connections, one interactive moment at a time. Also, who knew Worbla was basically magic?

21
DRAWING IN THE CROWD

The importance of engaging and interactive content

The next two weeks were a blur for Max and Mei. Inspired by their idols, they focused on building brands that truly showed their personality—Max adjusting his language to be more casual, like he was chatting with friends, and Mei deciding to be genuine without makeup, but act like the character she was inspired by when done up—she thought the cosplay aspect let her ride the line a little, and Max agreed it worked.

Their brands, and channels, built slowly, from 500 subscribers, to 600, and then 750. And that was fine! They weren't in it for overnight success. They were here for the long run, and that took time and hard work.

They met regularly, each excited to compare notes, ideas and advice. In particular, Mei was wondering how to engage with her budding audience, and it was with this in mind that they decided to attend a local fan convention. What better way to find out, as Max said, than to see what the experts did! The fact that the guy who did the voices for one of Max's favorite games was going to be there was just a… ah… happy coincidence.

Mei had laughed when he tried to slip that one past her. But… he was onto something with the audience engagement thing, even if he did have ulterior motives.

On the day of the event, Max and Mei stepped out of an uber and into what felt like the world's craziest, coolest live-action movie. A woman cosplaying as Batgirl wheeled a guy playing Professor X through the crowd. Captain America posed for photos with Pikachu, while Mario and Luigi could be seen buying books from a comic artist, and what felt like a hundred other different universes collided in a maelstrom of noise and sound.

"I think I'm in love," Max breathed.

"Me too."

They moved through the crowd, taking in the sights. A group of teens in matching T-shirts handed out flyers for their gaming channel, inviting people to participate in a live streaming event later that day. Mei took a flyer, admiring their enthusiasm.

As they continued to explore, they came across a booth with a large banner that read "Meet the Stars of Supernova Comics!" A line had already formed, and fans eagerly chatted with artists sitting at a collection of tables, who were drawing custom sketches and signing comic books. Max and Mei joined the line, watching as the artists engaged with each person, asking questions and making each interaction personal.

A woman with brightly colored hair looked up and smiled as they reached the front. "Hi there! What can I draw for you today?"

Max asked for a sketch of his favorite character, and as the artist drew, she chatted with them about their favorite comics and what they liked to do in their spare time. When she finished, she handed Max the sketch with a flourish.

"Here you go! Enjoy the rest of the convention!"

Max almost cried when he saw she'd sketched his hero sitting on a couch beside a bucket of popcorn, controller in hand. She'd been listening to him when he talked about what he loved.

"This... is the most beautiful thing I've ever seen," he murmured. He moved to kiss it, but then paused, putting it very carefully into his bag instead. "Don't want it to get lip marks," he murmured with a blush.

A group of cosplayers caught Mei's attention, and they headed in that direction. On the way they passed a workshop where kids were being taught how to draw their favorite comic characters. The instructor moved around, offering tips and encouragement, making each child feel special and valued. Max and Mei almost stopped, fascinated by how engaged the children were, but eventually decided to check it out later in the day.

Still, they couldn't help but marvel at all the various ways that the artists around them were connecting with their fans. Max and Mei had come here to learn about engagement, but hadn't realized just how easy, and varied, that could be. Whether through live

interactions, personalized sketches, or simply taking the time to talk, everyone they met seemed to have a knack for making others feel involved and appreciated.

It was an absolute buzz to watch, and Mei admitted to Max, a relief. She'd thought engaging with their viewers would be hard. But it wasn't! It was just... something they needed to remember to do.

22
COSPLAYERS ASSEMBLE!

How to make your audience feel welcomed and involved

Max and Mei soon found themselves amongst the cosplayers they'd seen earlier. The energy was infectious as fans crowded around, snapping photos and chatting with their favorite characters brought to life. A group of cosplayers seemed to be in the middle of an impromptu Q&A session. Mei steered them closer.

A cosplayer dressed as Captain Marvel was fielding questions from a starstruck teenager. "How long did it take you to make that suit?" she asked.

"About three months," she responded with a smile. "Lots of late nights and coffee, but it was worth it for everyone's reactions."

"For the bodysuit, I used a four-way stretch spandex. It's great because it fits snugly and moves with you, which is super important if you're going to be in costume all day. The gold accents are made from EVA foam—it's lightweight but holds its shape really well."

Max glanced at Mei, noting the spark in her eyes. She was soaking in every tip, not just as a fan but as someone thinking about how these techniques could apply to other creative projects.

Another fan, a boy with a backpack full of comic books, asked, "How did you get the emblem to look so realistic?"

"Ha!" Captain Marvel laughed. "That's all about layering." She touched the star emblem on her chest. "I started with a base of craft foam, then added layers with Worbla, which is a thermoplastic that you can heat and mold into shape. Once I it was shaped, I used metallic spray paint to give it that shiny finish."

Mei leaned in. "What about the boots?"

"Oh, those were actually an old pair I found at a thrift store," Captain Marvel said with a grin. "I painted them red with leather paint and added the gold details with vinyl. The key is to use flexible paint so that it doesn't crack when you walk."

Max watched, fascinated by how Captain Marvel broke down each part of the costume. The fans around them were equally engaged, asking about everything from the gloves to the wig. Captain Marvel wasn't just answering questions—she was connecting with people, making them feel involved in her journey.

They wandered toward a booth featuring cosplayers offering tips on how to create specific costume details. One of the cosplayers, dressed as Spider-Man, was showing a group of kids how to create the iconic webbing effect on his suit. The kids were mesmerized, their eyes wide with excitement as they tried the technique themselves, with Spider-Man offering encouragement and praise.

"They're really good at this," Max said, watching as the kids proudly showed off their work. "It's not just about the costume — it's about making the experience interactive."

Mei smiled. "Exactly. It's like they're inviting everyone to be a part of it. That's what makes it so fun."

They continued to explore the convention, but the interactions stuck with them. It wasn't just about the characters or the costumes. It was about creating a space where everyone felt involved, where fans weren't just watching but participating. The way the cosplayers made each interaction personal and engaging was something Max and Mei knew they could bring to their own content.

As the crowd dispersed, Max and Mei found a spot to sit.

"You know," Max said, pulling out his phone, "we should think about how to get our viewers involved like that. Not just leaving comments, but really making them a part of something."

Mei nodded, jotting notes in her book. "Yeah, engagement isn't just a strategy—it's the key to a loyal, interactive community."

She spotted a crowd gathered around a middle-aged man with a scruffy beard and ink-stained fingers. He looked just disheveled enough to be someone important. "Wanna check that out?"

Max nodded. "Let's do it."

23
TIME TO GET PRACTICAL

Practical ideas for audience participation

The middle-aged man with a scruffy beard and ink-stained fingers seemed to be some sort of artist. He stood at an easel, sketching out rough lines that quickly began to take the shape of a superhero in a dynamic pose. "Alright, who's got an idea for our hero's powers?" he asked the crowd.

A hand shot up. "What if he can control time?" called a young boy in a *Hulk Smash* jacket.

"Great idea!" the artist said, immediately adding a flowing clock to the hero's chest emblem. "Let's give him a costume that reflects that—maybe a cape that shifts like sand through an hourglass?"

As he continued to draw, more ideas flowed from the crowd—metallic gauntlets that could rewind or speed up time, boots that left trails of stardust, a mask with a shifting clock face. The artist incorporated each suggestion seamlessly, making the crowd feel like co-creators in the process.

Max and Mei exchanged glances. The artist wasn't just showing off his skills; he was involving the audience in a way that made them feel they were part of something special.

"This is so cool," Mei whispered. "It's like the whole crowd is working together with him."

Max nodded, captivated by the evolving character on the easel. The artist's hand moved swiftly, bringing the crowd's ideas to life. "He's making everyone feel like their ideas matter," Max observed quietly. "That's why everyone's so into it."

Mei had her notepad open. "We can totally use this to make our own channels better," she said, taking furious notes.

Max frowned. "I don't see how. I mean, maybe if I livestreamed, I could take suggestions. But most YouTube content is recorded ahead of time."

Mei didn't look up, her pencil still moving rapidly. "Maybe not exactly like this," she replied, her voice thoughtful. "Though you're right about livestreaming. You could invite viewers to join a game session, and I could have people follow along in a live tutorial."

She cocked her head, looking at what she'd written, then handed Max her notepad. A satisfied smile played across her lips. "That said, there are plenty of other practical ways we could encourage audience participation."

Max glanced at the list she'd created.

Polls and Surveys: Use polls to let viewers vote on upcoming content.

Q&A Sessions: Host live Q&A sessions where viewers can ask questions in real-time.

User-Generated Content: Start challenges where viewers can submit their own creations, like fan art or gameplay clips.

Contests and Giveaways: Run themed contests with fun prizes to engage viewers.

Max's eyes went wide as he read her ideas. "These are awesome," he said, his mind racing. "We could try out the polls first—ask people what they want to see next. And then maybe do a live Q&A to kick things off."

Mei grinned. "Exactly. It's not about just blindly following what this artist or Captain Marvel are doing. It's about the *spirit* of what they're trying to achieve, which is making the audience feel like they're part of the experience."

The crowd burst into applause as the artist wrapped up, cheering as he gave away the finished piece to Hulk Smash kid. Max and Mei walked away, their heads full of new ideas and possibilities. The artist's session had shown them that with the right approach, any audience could be more than just spectators— they could become participants in something much bigger.

24
FEEDBACK LOOP

Make viewers part of the creation process

Shortly after a food truck lunch of loaded nachos topped with cheese, and guacamole, Max and Mei slipped into a crowded panel room, grabbing seats near the front just as the lights dimmed.

On stage, seated comfortably with mic in hand, was the legendary voice actor Jack Silverman. One of the star attractions of the convention, he was known for voicing characters in some of the most popular games of the past decade. The room buzzed with excitement as Jack's deep, gravelly voice filled the auditorium.

"So, who here plays *Vortex Wars?*" Jack asked, grinning as nearly every hand in the room shot up. Max nudged Mei, his eyes wide with excitement. Vortex Wars was one of Max's top five favorite games. Hearing the voice of its iconic antagonist, Lord Nexus, was a dream come true.

Jack chuckled, leaning back in his chair. "You know, recording for Lord Nexus was one of the wildest experiences I've ever had. The director wanted the character to sound like he was speaking from the depths of a cosmic storm. So, they had me record while standing in a sound booth full of fans. And not the good kind that cheer you on, but literal fans, blowing in my face. It was like trying to deliver a monologue in a hurricane."

The audience laughed, drawn into Jack's story. With a playful grin, Jack added, "The fans—this time, the good kind—seemed to love it, so I guess the windburn was worth it."

Jack seemed to think of something. "Actually, want to know a secret?" he asked, leaning forward. "Lord Nexus' catchphrase, 'Bow before the storm' was inspired by a fan! They wrote in, saying how much they loved the idea of the villain being this unstoppable force of nature. So, we worked it in. It's a two-way street. You listen to your audience, you take what they give you, and you give something back that's even better."

Max nudged Mei. "He's so frikken cool! One day, when I'm famous, I swear I'm going to have him on my channel."

"Totally," murmured Mei. There was something powerful about the way Jack connected with his fans, not just as a performer but as someone who genuinely cared about their experience.

Jack delved into more stories about his time in the recording booth, and Max and Mei hung on his every word. The room was electric with anticipation, every attendee eager to hear the next behind-the-scenes nugget from a man who had brought some of their favorite characters to life.

"And let me tell you another thing," Jack said, leaning forward with a grin, "beta testing can make or break a game. Take *Vortex Wars* again. During the beta phase, the developers thought they had everything locked down. Lord Nexus was supposed to have this epic, galaxy-shattering ability—an attack that would basically one-shot the player if they didn't counter it in time."

He paused, eyes twinkling as he recalled the moment. "So, during one of the beta test sessions, the players were absolutely loving the game...until they hit that ability. They got wiped out left and right, no matter how good they were. And they weren't happy about it. The feedback poured in—people were frustrated, some even quit the beta altogether. It was a disaster."

Max and Mei leaned in closer, captivated by the story.

"The developers were initially set on keeping the ability as it was. They thought it added a challenge that would make the final victory even sweeter. But after seeing the overwhelming response from the testers, they realized they had to make a change. So, they tweaked the ability, gave players a small window to counter it with the right strategy. Suddenly, the game was balanced, and that same ability went from being a game-ender to a game-changer— something that made players feel powerful, rather than defeated."

Jack chuckled, shaking his head. "And here's the thing—Lord Nexus wouldn't be the iconic villain he is today if the developers hadn't listened. The beta testers' feedback didn't just improve the game; it shaped it. That's the power of listening to your audience. They're the ones who are experiencing your content firsthand, and sometimes they see things that you might not. Ignoring that feedback? That's like trying to play a game with your eyes closed."

Mei's pen was flying across her notepad now, capturing every word. Max could see the gears turning in her head, already planning how they could apply this to their own channels.

"That's the kind of connection we need to build with our viewers," Max whispered, half to himself. "If we give them a voice, they'll help us create something even better."

Jack finished his story with a smile. "Never underestimate the importance of feedback. It's not just about making tweaks—it's about making something that truly resonates with the people who matter most: your audience."

Max leaned back, the import of his hero's words hitting him just as hard as that one-shot Lord Nexus attack. The narrator had moved on to a story about having to hold a vibrating platform to get the right tremor in his voice for a character being electrocuted, but Max had stopped listening.

They'd been good at reading comments and taking feedback, but that story about the beta testers was different. Max and Mei needed to go further—to build a dialogue. To not just listen, but have a back-and-forth.

Max glanced at Mei, keen to tell her his revelation, but then saw her notepad. In huge letters and underlined, she'd written the words: *Make viewers an integral part of the creation process.*

It seemed she'd made the same connection.

25
STREAM TEAMS

Hosting a live event

Max and Mei closed out their day by attending a live stream hosted by YouTube fan favorite, Xander Blaze. Max had seen a couple of his streams before—his 'brand,' as he told Mei, centered around playing computer games in unique ways, such as the time he'd finished Elden Ring with an electric piano as a controller. The musical score of him defeating Malenia went viral after he worked *Mary had a Little Lamb* into his character's moveset.

The room buzzed with anticipation as fans settled into their seats, eyes glued to the massive screens on either side of the stage. Xander's setup was impressive: multiple cameras, microphones, a massive rear screen so the audience could see him play and a smaller dual-monitor system at front, so he could face the audience while he talked. Mei noticed a team of assistants discreetly managing the technical aspects of his show from the sidelines, and Max nodded. The dude had come prepared.

When Xander took the stage, the crowd erupted in applause.

He was magnetic, effortlessly drawing everyone in as he kicked off the event with live challenges that had both the online and in-room audience cheering and laughing. The first was a fan-favorite—Xander had to complete a near-impossible game level, but the twist was that the audience got to choose how he did it.

On stage, Xander unveiled a dance mat, guitar controller, electronic bongos, brainwave reader and more. The online poll he'd set up previously went nuts, with people shouting their ideas before quickly retrieving their phones to vote. Max and Mei joined in the mayhem, Mei voting that he complete the entire level using only voice command, while Max opted for a conventional controller, but Xander was only allowed to input commands with his nose.

Xander handled the rapidly updating poll results with ease, the results relaying in real time on the big screen behind him as he called out and encouraged the crowd. The dual screens before him must be showing his live chat, because occasionally he'd speak personally to someone who had messaged from home. Max thought the whole setup was seamless and incredibly professional.

Mei was just as engrossed, her eyes occasionally flicking to Xander's crew who were positioned around the stage, ready to jump in if needed. Xander made it look easy, effortlessly engaging with fans, calling out usernames, and responding to comments without missing a beat, but there had been a lot of work behind the scenes to make it look this good.

Even then, the show wasn't perfect. Halfway through, the audio cut out. As his backstage helpers plugged in cables and problem solved, Xander grinned at the camera. "Looks like the tech gods are having a little fun," he called, staying cool and calm. The crowd laughed, and when sound returned the event continued without a hitch.

The giveaways at the end were another highlight, with Mei and Max both leaping to their feet to vie for prizes. Most were fun and cheap, although the final prize was a custom gaming rig, courtesy of Xander's sponsor. Though neither Max nor Mei won, they weren't disappointed. They'd learned so much about their own channels by watching Xander that it was like they'd won first prize a hundred times over.

"That was something else," Max said as they walked from the room.

Mei nodded, notebook tucked under one arm. "Yeah, it really was. He's got it down to an art—everything just flowed."

They didn't need to spell it out; the lessons were clear. The planning, the preparation, the ability to roll with the punches— his show had been a masterclass in how to host a live event. And it wasn't just about the tech or the jokes either! Xander had created an experience that *looked* effortless, even though they knew how much work had gone into making it that way.

There were layers of preparation behind Xander's seamless performance: the backup equipment ready for any technical glitches, the carefully organized team managing the live chat, the structured flow of the event that kept everything on track, and the pre-planned interaction points that made the audience feel involved.

Making something look this effortless required meticulous planning, and *this* was the behind-the-scenes truth that Max and Mei took away. As they took the bus home from the convention, tired but exhausted, they couldn't wait to host their own live events.

With the right amount of preparation first, of course!

MEI'S NOTES:
ENGAGING WITH YOUR AUDIENCE

Engaging content is key
Whether it's live streams or regular videos, the more interactive and engaging the content, the more viewers feel involved. We need to ask questions, get feedback, and let our audience participate in shaping the content.

Make your audience feel welcomed
Just like the artist at the convention, acknowledging and interacting with viewers goes a long way in making them feel valued. Shout-outs, responding to comments, and live interactions create a stronger bond. We have to start doing this!!

Encourage participation
Create challenges, polls, and calls to action that make viewers want to engage. Whether it's a game challenge or asking viewers to send in their own creations, involving them directly makes the content feel personal.

Feedback helps us improve

The voice actor's story about beta testing taught us the importance of listening to audience feedback. It's not just about fixing things; it's about creating content that resonates with the people watching. In short, we need to make viewers an integral part of the creation process!

Live events are a whole different game

We learned that hosting live events or streams requires a lot of preparation - having a backup plan for tech issues, staying calm under pressure, and always keeping the energy up. It's about making the audience feel like they're part of something exciting and spontaneous.

Pro tip

Never wear boots with three-inch heels to a convention. My feet are still mad at me, but at least I looked amazing!

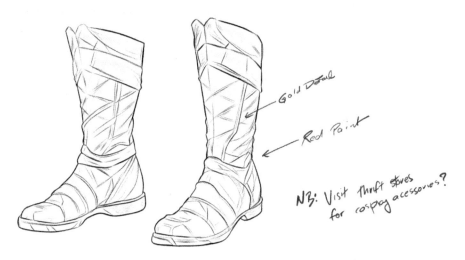

Gold Detail

Red Paint

NB: Visit thrift stores for cosplay accessories?

PART 6: CONSISTENCY IS KEY

In which our intrepid heroes learn that the secret to success lies in consistency—whether riding the waves or building a channel—and that sometimes the best advice comes with a side of roasted marshmallows.

26
THE SUN COMES UP EVERY DAY

The importance of regular content posting

The following Saturday, Max and Mei met at the local beach, both yawning but excited. The sun had barely risen, casting a soft glow over the water as they spotted the surfer girls already out on the waves, carving through the water with effortless precision. The air was crisp, and the sound of crashing waves mixed with the laughter of early risers scattered along the sand.

"Why is it so early?" Max complained, rubbing his eyes.

Mei laughed, nudging him. "This is when the good waves are."

Kaia, the girl they'd rescued at the café from the creep, paddled toward them, a wide grin on her face as she hopped off her board. "Morning, sleepyheads! Ready to catch some waves?"

Mei eyed the surfboard skeptically. "We'll watch for now."

Kaia shrugged, adjusting her wetsuit. "Suit yourselves. But you're missing out! We do this every morning—it's how we get better." She pointed to her fellow surfers, Lani and Piper, who were paddling out again. "You've got to show up, rain or shine."

Max raised an eyebrow. "Every single morning? Doesn't that get boring?"

Kaia shook her head, wiping seawater off her face. "Not at all. There's always something new to learn. Every wave's different, and you get better over time. It's like building muscle memory, or... I don't know, like running a YouTube channel."

Max and Mei perked up at that, intrigued.

Kaia continued, grabbing her board again. "I imagine if you only post once in a blue moon, people will forget about you, right? But if you're there regularly, even if the waves aren't perfect, people know you're serious. You keep showing up, they keep showing up."

Max nodded, watching Kaia paddle back out. "Makes sense," he said to Mei. "If you disappear for a while, your viewers move on. If you don't deliver, why would they hang around, right?"

Mei snorted, and Max looked over. "What?"

"Nothing," she said with a laugh. "Just, here I was thinking with over a thousand subs now, that we were getting good at this. Then Kaia just comes and schools us!"

Max burst out laughing. "Yeah. We're noobs. But hey, if the advice works..."

Mei nodded, leaning back into the sand. The girls showed up every day, no matter what the ocean threw at them. It was more than just surfing; it was a commitment, one that was slowly but surely paying off. They could learn from that.

27
IN SURF WE TRUST

Build trust with your audience

Max had just gotten comfortable, building himself a huge sand backrest, when Kaia exited the water scowling. Her surfboard had a huge crack running across the tip.

"No way," said Mei, standing up to inspect it. "The board looks almost new!"

Kaia sighed, running fingers over the damage. "It is. Well, it was." Her bottom lip pushed out as she made sad eyes at the board. "I'm out of the water until it's fixed."

Max, watching from his sandy throne, winced in sympathy. "That bad, huh?"

"One hundred," Lani said. "A cracked board can mess you up. You could wipe out, or worse, the board might snap completely."

Mei leaned in, examining the damage. "So, what do we do? How can we help?"

"Come with us to Paul's Surf Shack?" Kaia asked. She slung the board under her arm. "He's the only guy I trust to fix this up. Does amazing work every time. If we get it in now, we can be back out here by tomorrow."

Max raised an eyebrow. "You sound pretty confident about that."

Kaia jerked her head in the direction of the parking lot. They started walking. "Of course! Paul's been fixing our boards for ages. He does quality work, and he's never let us down. That's why we keep coming back."

The surf shop, a small wooden shack painted with waves and covered in surf stickers, was nestled just off the beach. Inside, the salty smell of ocean and wax filled the air, and the walls were lined with surfboards in various stages of repair. Paul, a sun-weathered man in his fifties, looked up from the counter as they walked in.

"Here to shake me down for money?" he asked Kaia, grinning as he nodded to a corner of the shop filled with super cool furniture. There were psychedelic sand chairs, graffitied beach umbrellas and even a custom painted surfboard. The Gyardos that coiled up its length looked almost alive. "I sold two chairs yesterday—can give you cash now, if you like."

Kaia grimaced. "Think I'll be using most of it on this," she said, handing over her board. "Cracked right down the middle. Can you work your magic?"

Paul inspected it, nodding thoughtfully. "It's a clean break. I can have it back to you by tomorrow, no problem."

"See?" Kaia said to Max and Mei. "Told you—Paul's the best. Never have to worry when he's on the job."

As Paul started gathering his tools, Max gestured to the furniture. "What's up with that?"

Kaia blushed. "You two might have… sort of… inspired me?" she said, scratching her head. "I've always loved upcycling furniture. When you guys said you just… you know… when you decided to start channels, *then went out and actually did it?* I figured it was time for me to stop talking about selling my stuff and actually do it. I asked Paul if I could rent a corner of his shop."

Mei had wandered over to the surfboard. "This stuff is awesome!" she said, admiring the paintjob. "You're so talented."

Kaia beamed. "Thanks! Piper, Lani and I paint a lot at the local graffiti park, but furniture is another thing entirely. Still, it paid for my board repair, so I'm happy!"

"And Paul does a good job?"

"Always," Kaia nodded.

Max bit his lip. "Makes sense, I guess. You go back to someone you trust because you know they'll do a good job every time."

Mei nodded, glancing around at all the boards waiting for repairs. "Yeah, consistency. It's like… if we keep delivering high-quality videos, people will trust us and keep coming back to watch more."

Max grinned. "So, we're basically like Paul, but for YouTube."

Lani overheard and laughed. "Just don't let your videos wipe out halfway through."

Max pretended to be wounded. "Hey, no wipe outs in my videos!" He scratched the back of his head. "Actually, that's not true. I wipe out all the time fighting bosses. *But*," he held up a finger. "I do it with style."

They all laughed, but Kaia's point resonated. Trust was earned by consistently delivering something good—whether it was a surfboard repair or a YouTube video. It wasn't about being flashy or perfect every time; it was about showing up and doing your best. And that, Max realized, was what kept people coming back for more.

28
SUIT UP AND STAND OUT

Stay committed to your brand

With the surfboard under repair, Max and Mei promised to return the next morning to help break it in. This time, though, there'd be no lounging on the beach! Kaia warned Max and Mei that they'd be joining her in the water.

"Um, I don't have a wetsuit," Max protested.

"Neither do I!" Mei echoed.

Kaia, Lani, and Piper exchanged mischievous glances. "Well then," they said with sly smiles, "looks like we're going shopping!"

They arrived at *Wave Riders*, shortly after, ferried by Kaia's older brother Jace in a beat-up combi van covered in surf stickers.

Calling their thanks as they spilled out the combi's big sliding doors, they stood before a colorful shop that looked straight from a beach in Hawaii. The exterior was adorned with murals of crashing waves and palm trees, and the windows displayed an array of surfboards and beachwear. They walked inside to find racks of wetsuits along one wall, as well as an impressive collection of board shorts, rash guards, and sun hats. The air smelled faintly of coconut sunscreen and neoprene.

"Alright, newbies," Piper said with a grin, "let's find you some gear that screams 'I belong on a board!'"

Max wandered over to a rack of wetsuits, his eyes widening at the variety. "Do I go for classic black, or is that too... basic?"

Lani laughed, pulling out a suit with bright blue accents. "Black's cool, but a little color never hurt anyone. Besides, it'll make it easier to spot you wiping out."

"Thanks for the vote of confidence," Max replied sarcastically, but he took the suit anyway.

Meanwhile, Mei was eyeing a coral-colored wetsuit with intricate wave patterns along the sleeves. "This is so pretty," she mused.

Kaia nodded approvingly. "That's totally you. It's important to pick something that reflects your style. When you feel good in your gear, it shows in your surfing."

Mei smiled, holding the suit up to herself. "I guess it's like expressing who you are, even out on the water."

"Exactly," Kaia agreed. "Your gear is part of your identity out there. It sets you apart."

Max emerged from the fitting room, striking a goofy pose in his wetsuit. "How do I look?"

"True to your identity," Piper said dryly. All the girls laughed.

They spent the next hour trying on gear, laughing at each

other's ridiculous poses, and offering opinions on everything from wetsuit colors to surfboard designs. The girls emphasized choosing items that not only fit well but also matched their personalities.

As they headed to the checkout, arms full of new gear, Max felt a newfound excitement. "I never realized how much thought went into this stuff," he said. "It's like you're creating your own brand."

"Well, yeah," Lani replied. "When we're out there, our style is part of who we are. It tells others what we're about without saying a word."

Mei pulled out her notebook, nodding thoughtfully. "Consistency in a style builds recognition. People know what to expect, and they trust you because of it."

She looked at Lani, and they both giggled. "Funny story, I once borrowed Lani's wetsuit," said Kaia. "I swear, half the beach got my name wrong that day!"

Everyone laughed as they exited the shop, agreeing to meet back up again tomorrow.

29
PRACTICE MAKES PERFECT

Improve through repetition

The following morning, Max and Mei once again arrived yawning at the beach, this time decked out in their brand-new wetsuits and ready to learn. The sky was just beginning to brighten, the early morning sun casting a soft glow over the water. Their friends were already out on the waves, effortlessly cutting through the water.

Max plopped down on the sand, stretching his legs out in front of him. "I could get used to this. Watching them surf while we wake up slowly? Best way to start the day."

Mei nodded, wrapping her arms around her knees as the salty air whipped through her hair. "Yeah, this is nice. Let's soak in the pro moves while we can."

Out on the water, the girls were taking turns trying new tricks. Kaia was working on a sharp cutback, turning her board smoothly back into the wave, while Lani was attempting to land a floater, riding up the crest of the wave before dropping back down.

Lani didn't quite nail it on her first few attempts. Her board slipped out from under her, sending her crashing into the wave with a splash. Max winced but couldn't help grinning. "Oof, that looked rough."

Lani popped back up, laughing and shaking the wet hair from her eyes. She paddled back into position, undeterred.

"It's like she's not even fazed by falling," Mei muttered. "She just keeps going back."

"Gotta respect the persistence," Max agreed.

This time, Lani came closer to landing the trick, staying on her board for a second longer before wiping out. Still, there was no frustration, no hesitation—just a determination to try again.

"Repetition," Mei said thoughtfully. "I guess that's how you get better at anything, right? Like with our channels."

Max nodded, eyes never leaving Lani's board. "Yeah, I guess so. Every time we film, we improve a little—learn what works, what doesn't."

Lani finally nailed the floater, riding the crest of the wave with grace before dropping back down to cheers from her friends. Max leapt to his feet, hooting and hollering from the beach.

The surfers all rode whitewash back to shore, Lani grinning at their congratulations. "I just keep going until I get it," she said as she walked up. She raked fingers through her hair. "It's all about putting in the work."

Mei grinned ruefully. "Makes me think about all the times we've scrapped videos because they didn't feel right. Maybe we should keep going with them, learn as we go."

Lani shrugged. "I've never done it, but I guess if a video isn't perfect, every attempt would get you better? It's like surfing—you're building muscle memory for your channels."

Then her eyes narrowed. "But that's enough of that," she said with a mischievous grin. "It's your turn to get wet!"

30
CATCH THAT WAVE!

Maintaining momentum

Max stood knee-deep, staring at the rolling waves with wide eyes. "So... we just jump on the board and hope for the best?"

Kaia chuckled. "Not exactly. The trick is to paddle hard enough to catch the wave, then once you're on it, lean forward and commit. If you hesitate and lose momentum, the wave will pass you by."

They paddled out a little farther, the ocean swelling beneath them. Kaia kept close, explaining when to paddle harder and when to ease off. Every time a wave approached, Max felt a rush of excitement (and fear!) as he paddled furiously. But time after time, the wave passed him by before he could catch it.

"You're not fully committing," Kaia said, waiting for him to get back on his board after a failed attempt. "You're hesitating right when you should be pushing harder. Once you catch the wave, you need to trust it to carry you and keep the momentum going."

Max groaned, frustrated. "I'm trying, but every time I feel like I'm almost there, I mess up."

Mei, floating nearby, had just finished riding a small wave before wiping out with a big grin on her face. "You're overthinking it, Max," she said, pushing her hair out of her eyes. "It's like our videos—if we stop every time something doesn't go perfectly, we'll never get anywhere. But if we just keep going, we'll stay on track. You've got to trust the process."

Max blinked, letting the words sink in. "Just keep going, huh?"

Mei nodded, her soaked face beaming. "Exactly. Trust it."

With Mei's words bouncing around his head, Max turned back to the ocean, determined. He watched the waves carefully, feeling their rhythm, and when the next one came, he paddled hard, trusting the wave to carry him. This time, he didn't hesitate.

Before he knew it, the wave lifted him. The board wobbled beneath his feet, but he leaned forward, keeping his balance as he surfed toward the shore, the wind whipping past his face.

The thrill of it hit him like a rush. He wasn't just riding a wave—he was moving with it, keeping his balance, staying in motion. For those brief seconds, he was completely in the flow.

When he wiped out, he came up laughing.

Kaia paddled over, clapping him on the back. "See? You kept your momentum and trusted the wave. That's the key."

Mei paddled closer. She was grinning. "Told you."

Max nodded, still buzzing. This felt waaay better than sitting on the beach.

31
S'MORE PLANNING

Setting a content schedule

The sun had dipped below the horizon, casting warm oranges and purples across the sky as Max, Mei, and their new friends sat around a crackling bonfire. The waves lapped gently at the shore, providing a rhythmic soundtrack to their laughter and chatter. Kaia, Lani, and Piper were huddled close to the fire, roasting marshmallows and recounting stories of past surfing trips. Max and Mei, wrapped in beach towels, sat nearby, still buzzing from their day of learning how to surf.

Lani stretched her legs toward the warm fire, sighing contentedly. "Today was epic," she said. "Those waves were just perfect."

Kaia grinned, toasting a marshmallow. "See? Told you waking up early was worth it."

Max chuckled. "I have to admit, I wasn't thrilled about the 5 a.m. alarm, but you were right."

Mei pulled her towel tighter around her shoulders. "I didn't realize how much planning goes into surfing."

"What do you mean?" asked Piper.

"Well," Mei continued, "I thought surfers just showed up at the beach and caught waves whenever. But you gals check tides, winds, all that stuff."

Kaia shrugged. "You kinda have to. The ocean's always changing. Knowing the conditions helps us catch the best waves."

Lani nodded. "Yeah, you can't just paddle out anytime and expect great surf. Timing is everything."

Max poked at the fire with a stick. "Makes sense."

Piper tossed him a marshmallow. "How do you handle your YouTube channels?" she asked. "Just wing it, or is there some master plan?"

Max exchanged a glance with Mei. "Uh, we mostly just post videos whenever we finish them," he admitted.

Lani raised an eyebrow. "No schedule? How do your fans know when to expect new content?"

Mei shrugged, a bit sheepish. "We haven't really thought about that. We just upload when we can."

Kaia poked the fire, sending a swirl of sparks into the night sky. "Wow. If we showed up at the beach randomly, we'd miss the best waves or get low tide. Pretty cool you don't have to plan your content."

Max rubbed the back of his head. "Umm. I'm kinda wondering now if we should?"

Mei's eyes lit up. "It *would* help us stay consistent. *And* we wouldn't feel so rushed all the time. We could even plan videos around upcoming events!"

Kaia grimaced. "Sorry."

Max sighed. "No, you're right. We *should* get more organized. It's just... so much extra work."

Mei shook her head. "Wrong." She held up a stick covered in marshmallow. "Not about getting more organized. We totally need a content calendar," she said quickly. "But about it being more work. There'd actually be less. Just, some of it would be frontloaded."

Max narrowed his eyes. "Explain." He side-eyed the marshmallow bag. "Also, hit me."

Piper threw him two. He popped one in his mouth, and another on his stick.

"Well," said Mei. "It's like this." She turned to Piper. "If you didn't look up the best times to surf, and when you arrived the water was glassy, what would you do?"

Piper shrugged. "Go home. Sulk. Come back when there *is* surf."

"And, would that be more, or less work than just looking up a wave chart?"

"Totally more work!"

"Sooo," said Mei, turning back to Max. "If you create a gameplay video, and it bombs because the next Zelda just released and nobody's playing anything else for the next month, would that waste of time be more or less work than planning out a calendar with when games release, then tying your videos into that?"

"Yoo maag a goob poid."

"What was that?"

Max swallowed his marshmallow. "You make a good point!" He laughed. "Let's do it."

Kaia raised her marshmallow stick like a toast. "To planning ahead and surfing like a pro—be that in the ocean, or online!"

They all laughed, tapping their sticks together before roasting more marshmallows. The conversation shifted to funny stories about past surfing mishaps, and the atmosphere eased into comfortable camaraderie.

As the stars twinkled overhead and the fire crackled softly, Max leaned back with a contented sigh. "This turned out to be a pretty awesome day," he said.

Mei nodded, smiling as she gazed into the flames. "Yeah, it really did."

MEI'S NOTES:
CONSISTENCY IS KEY

Create a content schedule
Planning isn't about losing creativity, it's about staying consistent and prepared. Having a content schedule helps us avoid last-minute stress and keep the momentum going.

Consistency builds trust
It's like Paul taking care of Kaia's surfboard - he delivered consistent quality and kept her coming back. If Paul started promising to fix her board in a day, but then closed his shop and didn't open it for another two weeks, do you think Kaia would ever come back?

Planning ahead reduces stress later
Front-loading effort by scheduling content makes things smoother down the line. Unless we really want to build videos that nobody wants to view, all because of events we could have clearly seen coming? *Note to self: prep videos for holidays and special events. Maybe do a Halloween makeup special?*

Momentum is everything!

Just like riding a wave, we can't stop once we've caught it - we need to keep going, even if it feels tough.

Repetition makes us better

Well, not Max. He insists he's already perfect ;| But seriously, even if we mess up, the more we create content the more we improve. Consistency builds skills over time.

Commit to the brand

Our channels should reflect who we are, just like how the girls' wetsuits and boards match their personalities. Staying true to that helps people recognize and connect with us. Another way to put it? We need to be consistent both with *how* often we post, and in the *style* of what we post.

Develop a posting schedule

The best YouTubers never miss a release date. Their audiences know and trust them to produce content on time, every time.

Fun Fact

Max actually managed to catch a wave - after I told him to stop overthinking. Maybe I should start charging for my advice!

PART 7: MASTERING THE ALGORITHM

In which our intrepid heroes uncover that mastering algorithms isn't about tricks or shortcuts—it's about understanding your audience, delivering quality, and keeping them clicking for more. Also, Cuthbert the peace lily might just outgrow them all.

32
ROBOT WARS!

Quality over quantity
Consistency

Max and Mei continued their surfing lessons in and around school, homework, and, most importantly, expanding their YouTube channels. Each time they met, it seemed like there was something new to learn or some strategy to apply. They were busy! But it was the kind of busy that filled them with excitement because they were making progress toward their goals. With their high quality and highly engaging videos now also highly consistent, their subscriber numbers rocketed upwards in leaps and bounds, jumping from 1,000 to 1,500 and then 2,500 in under a month. Max had experienced a dip right in the middle that had them both worried, but he'd bounced back without too much damage.

Pouring so much effort into making YouTube a serious business didn't come without drawbacks. After several weeks of exhausting work, they decided they needed a break. And Max knew just the thing—news of a cool outdoor tech fair had popped up in his feed. "It's not just techy stuff," Max said with a grin. "There's robot-building booths, virtual reality games, and who knows what else!"

Mei raised an eyebrow. "Robots, really? That's not exactly my thing."

Max grinned. "What if we build two robots and make them fight, robot wars-style?"

Mei laughed. "Do I get to name them?

Max nodded.

"I'm in."

The fair was a buzz of activity. Booths stretched in every direction, with tech enthusiasts, inventors, and curious onlookers crowding around displays of futuristic gadgets. Max and Mei wandered through the maze of excitement until they found the **Build-Your-Own Robot** booth, complete with tables covered in wires, gears, and plastic parts. Several robots buzzed around, giving off a whir of mechanics.

"Alright," Max said, grabbing two sets of robot parts. "We're making fighters. Let's see who builds the ultimate battle bot!"

They started construction quickly, giving the instructions only the most cursory of glances. How hard could it be? The motor connected to the drive shaft, and the... uh, servo to the chassis?

"We're gonna finish these in record time," Max said, eyeing a shiny set of wheels. "Then, robot wars!"

Within minutes, they had two robots that, to be honest, looked

pretty impressive. Mei chuckled as she painted quick faces on them. "Meet BB-H8 and R2-D2.0," she said, holding them up proudly.

Max grinned. "Alright, let's see them fight!"

Mei hit the power buttons, and... both robots twitched once before falling apart.

"What just happened?" Max asked, face falling.

The booth operator walked over, shaking his head with a smile. "Looks like you rushed through it. Try again but focus on building it right. Quality is what counts—two robots aren't going to do much if they can't stay in one piece."

Max sighed but nodded. He and Mei got back to work, this time following the steps more carefully. They checked every part, making sure each wire was secure, and spent time making sure the robots were sturdy. The battle idea took a backseat as they focused on getting just one robot right.

As they worked, Mei paused, her hands steadying a wire. "This kind of reminds me of our YouTube channels. Like, we're pumping out videos consistently now, but if didn't make them good, people would stop watching."

Max grimaced. "Don't remind me." A couple of weeks ago, he'd kinda... coasted through a couple of videos. Family commitments meant he hadn't had as much time as he liked, and even though he *knew* the sound on one of them wasn't great, and a second needed serious editing, he'd pushed them out just to be consistent.

He'd lost subscribers on both those videos, and only kept his upward trend going with some serious effort—and a lot of help from Mei. "It's like what's the point of having two robots—or 20 videos—if none of them can do what they're supposed to?" he muttered.

After what felt like forever—but was probably only 30 minutes—their robot was finally complete. This time, when Mei pressed the button, the robot whirred to life, rolling forward smoothly. The anime face she'd painted on it grinned up at them.

Max grinned back. "Now that's a quality bot."

The booth operator gave them a nod. "Consistency, and quality over quantity. Doesn't matter how many robots—or videos—you make, if they're not solid."

Max scrubbed the back of his head with a chuckle. "Yeah. Figured that out the hard way."

33
THE CLICKBAIT TRAP

Understanding your audience
Thumbnails
Titles

It only took fifteen minutes to build the second robot. Once Max and Mei knew what they were doing, they worked faster while still keeping quality high. Mei's mecha won their robot battle, much to Max's chagrin. She demanded churros as payment.

While searching for the delicious deep-fried lines of sugary goodness, Max and Mei wandered into a bustling area of the tech fair filled with bright lights and catchy music. One stall immediately grabbed Max's attention. It was decked out in flashing neon signs proclaiming, **"UNBELIEVABLE PRIZES!"** and **"EVERYONE'S A WINNER!"** The walls were plastered with images of the latest gadgets and gaming consoles.

"Whoa, look at that!" Max exclaimed. "Wanna give it a shot?"

Mei eyed the stall warily. "I don't know... It seems a bit much."

"But think of the prizes!" Max argued. Before she could protest,

Max handed over cash and received a token. Lights flashed, bells rang, and the machine spun dramatically. Finally, it stopped, and a small compartment opened, revealing a cheap plastic whistle.

Max picked it up, his excitement deflating. "Seriously?"

The vendor shrugged. "Better luck next time!"

As they walked away, Max sighed. "All that hype for a plastic whistle. Talk about misleading."

"Yeah," Mei agreed. "They sure know how to catch your eye, but they don't deliver."

They continued exploring and soon came across another booth. This one was simple yet inviting. A clear sign read, **"Design Your Own Buttons!"** with colorful examples neatly displayed. People were gathered around, happily creating personalized buttons.

"This looks cool," Mei said, her interest piqued.

They approached, and the attendant greeted them warmly. "Care to make your own custom button?"

"Definitely!" Max replied.

They spent the next twenty minutes designing and crafting buttons to pin to their jackets.

Mei experimented with various stickers and colors, but after piling on a bunch of decals, eventually frowned. "Too cluttered."

Removing them, she drew two makeup brushes with thick black lines, crossed so the tips formed angelic wings. A dab of teal and gold to contrast the black, and she was done. "Better."

Max looked over. "Nice—could almost be your logo! The

contrast makes it pop." He showed her his own button, a robot silhouetted against a red background. "Originally I went into a whole lot of detail. But I think this works better."

Mei nodded. Simplifying the design made it much more eye-catching. "I guess sometimes less really is more," she agreed.

They were both delighted with the results, proudly pinning the buttons to their jackets as they left.

"That was awesome," Max said. He nodded meaningfully in the direction that he'd gained the plastic whistle. "And they didn't need a bunch of flashy signs to get us interested."

Mei smiled. "They showed us exactly what we'd get, and it was worth it."

Max nodded thoughtfully. "I guess sometimes keeping it simple and honest works best."

Mei glanced back at the crowded button booth. "People appreciate knowing what they're getting into."

Just then, the enticing aroma of cinnamon and sugar caught their attention.

"Speaking of getting what you want," Mei nudged him, "you still owe me that churro."

Max laughed. "And here I was hoping you'd forget!"

34
KEEPING THE CROWD CLAPPING

Audience retention
Engagement

A quick detour to the food trucks and several cinnamon-sugar-coated fingers later, they found themselves wandering back into the heart of the tech fair. The sound of laughter and music caught their attention as they approached a crowd gathered around a man with a guitar. He was switching between songs and cracking jokes, and the audience was mesmerized.

"Let's check this out," Max said, edging closer.

The man on stage called out as they arrived. "You two!" he point to them with a grin. "Give me a topic for the next song."

Mei blinked in surprise, then blurted "Makeup!"

Max snorted. "Video games!" he added.

The performer didn't miss a beat. He strummed his guitar and launched into an improvised tune, singing about a tube of lipstick with stats so high barbarians wore it as armor. The crowd roared with laughter, Max and Mei laughing with them.

As the song went on, the performer made quick adjustments, taking cues from the audience's reactions. A groan when the joke fell flat? He switched it up. A louder cheer? He leaned into it, letting the energy guide him.

Mei elbowed Max. "He's really good at reading the crowd."

"Yeah," Max replied, nodding. "Knows just when to switch things up. Never stays on one bit for too long."

The crowd was hooked—clapping and laughing. The performer played off their energy, making jokes, changing rhythms, and even pausing to let the audience shout out suggestions. It was like watching someone orchestrate chaos with perfect precision.

As they laughed along with the crowd, Max noticed how the performer had a natural rhythm to his act, adjusting when needed but always keeping the crowd on board. They weren't just watching a show—they were part of it. He nudged Mei. "We need to get people involved like this guy does."

"Yeah," Mei agreed, eyes still on the performer. "It makes everything way more fun."

When the performer wound up, the crowd chanted for more. Max and Mei lingered, caught in the energy of it all. It was clear— the way he kept everyone hooked, drawing them in and making them part of the act, was exactly why no one wanted to leave.

Max and Mei joined the chant. The man grinned, then strummed his guitar and acquiesced, playing one last song.

35
BALLOONING ISSUES

Patience & Adaptability
Encouraging interaction

Leaving the guitarist behind, Max and Mei found themselves moving from the lively, buzzing crowd to a quieter section of the tech fair. It was a strange contrast—just moments ago, they'd been in the middle of a cheering mass, but now, they stood by a balloon artist who, despite his brightly colored setup, struggled to attract much attention.

The artist, dressed in a futuristic jumpsuit covered in LED lights, was trying his best. He twisted balloon creations at lightning speed—hovering drones, tech-themed hats, even a balloon robot—but only a handful of people seemed interested.

"Poor guy," Mei said softly. "That's gotta be rough."

Max nodded. "Yeah, it's like no one even notices him."

They stood back, watching for a while. The artist kept trying, adjusting his routine, occasionally calling out to passersby. But the more he struggled, the less attention he got.

"I feel bad," Max muttered. "He's putting in all this effort, but... I don't know."

Suddenly, the balloon artist spotted Max and Mei hovering nearby. He waved them over with a grin, clearly happy to have some attention. "Hey there! Want to see the latest in balloon technology?"

Max and Mei exchanged glances but shrugged, stepping closer.

The artist lit up—literally. His jumpsuit pulsed with a rainbow of colors as he rapidly twisted a balloon into what looked like a tiny robot. He handed it over to Max with a flourish. "This is ProcrastinaBot," he said with a wink. "It's perfect for guarding all the things you promised to do later." Max chuckled, turning the balloon robot over in his hands. "This is pretty cool."

As the artist worked on a larger creation—a balloon drone, complete with spinning propellers—Max noticed that he was getting better at drawing people in. His jokes were sharper, and he started calling out more directly to passersby, explaining what made his balloon creations different.

It took time, but eventually, a small crowd began to gather. Mei watched, impressed. "He's adjusting," she whispered. "He's figuring out what works."

Max nodded. "Yeah, he didn't give up even when no one was paying attention."

The crowd started to grow as more people stopped to watch the balloons take shape. The artist had found his rhythm, cracking jokes and engaging people as he worked. His persistence was paying off.

As they walked away, Max glanced back at the balloon artist, now surrounded by an excited group of kids marveling at his creations. The once-empty corner had transformed into a hub of laughter and curiosity. "You know," Max said, spinning the balloon robot in his hands, "it's kind of cool to see someone turn things around like that. He started slow, but now look at him—he's killing it."

Mei smiled, watching as the artist high-fived a kid holding a balloon drone. "Yeah. It's not about starting perfect; it's about figuring it out as you go. He found his crowd."

Max nodded. "Makes me think about our channels. Even though things are going okay, there's always room to improve—try new things, see what connects better."

Mei glanced at the little balloon robot Max was still holding. "Exactly. Sometimes all it takes is a twist in the right direction."

They shared a grin, stepping back into the buzzing energy of the tech fair, both a little more inspired to keep their own momentum going.

36
CUTHBERT THE PEACE LILY

Viewer engagement
Watch time

Max and Mei continued wandering through the tech fair, their excitement building with each new exhibit they passed. Neon-lit gadgets, holograms, and interactive displays pulled them in all directions, but it was the next booth that really caught their attention. A group of people stood around what looked like... plants. Regular, everyday houseplants, but hooked up to small cameras and screens displaying social media feeds.

Max squinted, not believing his eyes. "Does... that plant have a Facebook account?" he asked incredulously.

A man in a lab coat smiled. "And a YouTube channel." He pointed to a row of four lush green plants, each in its own sealed glass tank. ""Each plant has a webcam. People from all over the world can log in, watch the plants grow, and interact with them. But here's the twist—the only way they get watered is through likes and comments."

Mei's eyes widened. "That's... kinda crazy. So, if nobody likes the plant, it doesn't get any water?"

"Exactly," the scientist confirmed, gesturing to the largest tank, where a gorgeous peace lily was flowering. "Take Cuthbert, for example. When we first set up the experiment, he wasn't getting much attention. Hardly any likes, hardly any water. We had to come up with ways to get people to engage more."

Max raised an eyebrow. "Cuthbert?"

The scientist chuckled. "Yeah, we got creative. Gave it a name, made the plant's feed more interesting, even put googly eyes on it. Once people started getting invested, engagement went through the roof. Cuthbert went from surviving to thriving."

Max and Mei exchanged looks. "That's amazing."

The scientist rubbed his head. "Nah, the amazing thing is that it's compounding. The more people interact with the plants, the bigger the plant grows. The bigger the plant grows; the more people watch and give it likes."

Max leaned closer to the tanks, observing a tiny drop of water hit a leaf. Someone halfway across the world had just liked it. "You've cracked the code," he said in a whisper.

The scientist shrugged. "I don't know about that. But I do know it's about more than just getting people to your page," he said. "It's about getting them to hang around after they've shown up. The more time someone spends watching Cuthbert here, the more likely they are to give it water."

"And they come back?"

The scientist nodded. "With friends! Once we've got some watch time on a video, and viewer engagement, YouTube's algorithms take over." He hesitated. "You know about algorithms, right?"

Max nodded. "It's how YouTube decides which videos to show more often."

The scientist nodded. "Correct. It's a formula developed by analyzing millions of viewers' behaviors to predict what they're most likely to want to watch next, based on their actions," he said. "In our case, the formula sees people interacting with Cuthbert and thinks he must be important, so it shows him more frequently in stranger's feeds. And that leads to more views. Which leads to more screentime. It's compounding."

He held up a finger. "*If* you do it right. Like I said, it's about more than just getting people to the page. They have to stick around. Interact. Be engaged."

Max shook his head, still trying to process what he'd just seen. "Who knew plants could teach us so much about growing our YouTube chan…" He trailed off, eyes wide as he saw the plant's subscribers. Cuthbert had more views than them both combined!

Mei just laughed, pulling out her phone to give Cuthbert a drink.

37
THE INVENTOR'S WORKSHOP

Being genuine
SEO basics

The tech fair was starting to wind down, but Max and Mei weren't done exploring. They wandered toward the outskirts, where a booth titled *Stall #82* caught their eye. Unlike the sleek, polished setups they'd seen earlier, this one was a chaotic jumble of wires, blinking lights, and half-finished gadgets.

"Whoa," Max whispered. "It's like a mad scientist's lab."

A wild-haired inventor buzzed around the booth, talking to himself as he adjusted various devices. On one side a contraption was automatically flipping through comic book pages—until it hit a staple and the entire mechanism froze, tossing the comic onto the ground with a sad whirr. The inventor frowned, fiddling with it. "Still working out the kinks," they heard him mutter.

On another table, a clunky machine stood wobbling. "This," the inventor declared proudly when they approached, "is my self-folding laundry machine—except right now it thinks folding means turning shirts into paper planes. Not efficient, but fun at parties."

Max and Mei stifled laughs as they continued exploring the booth. The place was filled with oddities like a pencil-sharpening helmet, a 'sprinkle cannon' designed to speed-coat ice cream, and a device that whistled every time someone approached it.

Then the inventor pointed to a tangle of tubes connected to a plant pot. "Ah, my smart watering system! It adjusts watering based on moisture levels—perfect for people who can't keep plants alive!"

Mei perked up. "Hey, that'd be great for Cuthbert!" They explained the plant they'd met at the Social Experiment booth.

The inventor blinked in surprise. "Really? Well, I hadn't thought of that. I'll be sure to reach out."

Max and Mei continued to look around. Despite the booth's fascinating inventions, they had the stall entirely to themselves. Most people barely gave it a glance before moving on, confusion on their faces.

Max frowned, mentioning the issue to Mei.

She nodded. "It's like no one knows what anything is." Turning to the inventor, she waved him over. "Excuse me. Have you ever thought about labelling some of this stuff? It would give people an idea of what they're looking at. Maybe even have a short description or something."

The inventor snapped his fingers. "Ah, like people do for

YouTube thingies? You know, with the titles and... what do they call them?"

"Tags?" offered Max. "Keywords? SEO?" SEO stood for Search Engine Optimization. It wasn't something he did personally, but he understood the concept of using describing words to make things easy to find when people searched online.

"Yes!" enthused the inventor. "That's what I meant. Are you YouTubers?"

"We are!" replied Mei proudly.

The inventor whistled. "You must know a thing or two. Got any advice? If people knew what my stuff was about, I bet a lot more people would stick around."

Max shifted his weight from one foot to the other, crossing his arms. "Umm..." He hesitated for a second, then glanced to Mei.

His friend grimaced. "Yeah... we aren't really practicing what we preach right now? Our current strategy all boils down to *throw-spaghetti-at-wall-and-hope-something-sticks.*" She gave a self-depreciating chuckle. "'Cosplay Makeup Look #2' isn't exactly a magnet for clicks."

"Oh," said the inventor. "Looks like we all have some homework. But you think labelling my inventions is a good place to start?"

Max nodded. He'd been thinking while Mei spoke. "You know what? I think so! Maybe even a get a new sign for the stall? Number 82 doesn't really tell people much."

The inventor scratched his cheek, thinking Max's words through. "What would you suggest?"

"Figure out what people are searching for," Max suggested. "Like, what words would help people looking for this stuff know it was here if they read the sign?"

The inventor's eyes lit up. "Search terms! Oh, that's easy then." He gestured expansively, spreading his hands like he was visualizing a the sign before him. "*Ice cream!*"

Mei and Max went quiet, puzzling through the inventor's words. Looking around, Max cleared his throat. "Um..." he said delicately. "Are you giving away ice cream somewhere?"

"The sprinkle cannon!"

"Does it *actually* make ice cream though?"

The inventor shook his head. "No, just coats it with sprinkles really, really fast. But I figure anyone that likes ice cream would want it, right?"

"Riiight," Max said slowly. He grimaced. "But here's the thing. If you say *ice cream* on your sign, you'll get people expecting ice cream at your stall. You'll actually do more damage if they come here then don't get it, than not having a sign at all."

"Oh. So... no ice cream?" asked the inventor.

Mei took pity on him. "It was a good idea, but you have to be honest about what you say." She searched for how to explain it. "Think about what you have in your booth, and then think about what people would have to see on a sign to find it."

"Exactly!" Max said. "Like, with my YouTube videos, I can't just lie and title my video 'World of Warcraft' if it's about a Zelda title. But after that, I want to get specific. 'How to get the master sword in Breath of the Wild' is way better than my usual 'Episode 83'. It tells people exactly what they're getting, and it's something I'd search for if I was looking for that video."

Max snapped his fingers at Mei. "Actually, can you write that title down for me, please? It's brilliant!"

Mei gave him a look. But eventually, she sighed and pulled out her notebook.

When she'd written down his next title video—he so owed her more smoothies for that—she nodded to the inventor. "For you, maybe a sign like 'the inventors workshop' would be good for your stall? And then something like, 'The Ultimate Plant-Watering Gadget for Forgetful Gardeners,' as a label under the water pot. You know, make it clear what people are getting into, but also make it exciting so people want to see it!"

Max glanced at the tangle of wires and blinking lights on the inventor's table. "Honestly, this stuff's incredible. If people knew what half of it was, they'd be lining up to see it."

The inventor rubbed his chin, a thoughtful smile spreading across his face. "Guess I've got my next project, then."

As they walked away, Mei smirked and elbowed Max. "You know, for two people handing out advice on SEO, we're not exactly crushing it ourselves."

Max laughed, rubbing the back of his neck. "Yeah, 'Episode 83' really screams 'must watch,' doesn't it?" He shook his head, half amused, half embarrassed. "Guess we've got our own spaghetti-wall situation to fix."

Behind them, the inventor's muttering drifted through the air. "A machine to generate keywords... now that's an idea!"

MEI'S NOTES:
MASTERING THE ALGORITHM

YouTube's algorithm is like a super-smart program that decides which videos to show people based on what they like and watch. Nobody but Google knows exactly how it works, but there are some things my research says can help it notice our videos:

- Using the right keywords so YouTube knows what our videos are about.
- Getting people to click on our videos.
- Keeping them watching once they've clicked.
- Getting people to comment, like, and subscribe.

Max and I learned a ton from the tech fair about how to make this happen! We put our heads together and brainstormed over churros, and came up with a bunch of ways we can influence YouTube's algorithm in our favor:

Be consistent
Like building that robot, sticking to a schedule is key. If we keep making great videos regularly, YouTube sees that we're reliable and shows our stuff to more people.

Quality over quantity
Remember how the rushed robots fell apart? It's better to post fewer amazing videos than loads of average ones. If people stay longer because our videos are good, YouTube notices that!

Thumbnails that pop
We learned from the button-making booth that simple and eye-catching works best. If our thumbnails stand out, more people will click on them. Also, I read somewhere that people like seeing reactions - it's more personal. Maybe tell Max to start featuring his face doing funny reactions in his thumbs?

Be real
People trust authenticity. Sure, we got suckered once (well, Max did) at the carnival game, but we're never going back! We will do more buttons if we ever see them again though - that place rocked! Basically, if we're honest and genuine in our videos, our audience will stick around - and YouTube will notice.

Titles that make sense

The inventor reminded us that clear labels are everything. If we name our videos things people actually search for, we're more likely to get noticed.

Know your audience

The street performer nailed it by reading the crowd. If we focus on what our viewers love - whether its makeup looks inspired by Zelda or beginner game tips - we'll keep them coming back.

Keep them watching

The performer didn't just hook people - he kept them glued to his act. If our videos are engaging all the way through, we'll boost our watch time, which helps YouTube recommend us more.

Ask for interaction

Cuthbert the Peace Lily thrived because people got involved by liking and commenting. We need to do the same - ask questions, respond to comments, and keep people engaged.

Watch time is gold

The more time people spend watching, the more YouTube thinks, "this is good stuff," and shows our videos to more people.

Be adaptable

The balloon artist reminded us that things don't always go to plan. Being patient and tweaking what we do can make all the difference in keeping our channel growing.

SEO basics

Using good keywords, tags, and descriptions is like putting a sign on your booth that says exactly what's inside. Seriously, this one is really important. YouTube searches through everything you write (like a title, or description) to try and see if what you've got is what someone else wants to see. The more describing words we supply, the better our chances YouTube will have to recommend our stuff!

Max's homework

"How to get the master sword in Breath of the Wild"- great title for Max's next video.

My homework

"How to start using your own notebook and also you owe me a smoothie"- great title for my next convo with Max!

PART 8: HANDLING CRITICISM AND TROLLS

In which our intrepid heroes discover that trolls are just creepers waiting to blow up their builds, but constructive feedback? That's like upgrading your armor to diamond.

38
CREEPERS IN THE COMMENTS

Constructive criticism vs. trolling

Energized by the tips and tricks they'd picked up at the Tech Fair, Max and Mei dove headfirst into experimenting with their videos. They fine-tuned their keywords, made their thumbnails pop, and found new ways to engage with their audience—all in an effort to catch YouTube's attention.

And it worked! Almost overnight, their videos started gaining traction. Their subscriber count shot up, climbing by almost 500 subscribers per week to 4,000. They were even getting close to monetization, though they hadn't yet achieved the watch hours needed to get over the line. Max and Mei hoped that would come their way soon.

Unfortunately, more views also meant more opinions, and not all of them were positive.

"Your videos are so boring. No one cares about makeup. Get a life."

Mei sat back, chewing her lip. They'd been scrolling through the comments on her latest video, and she'd been feeling so good! Then out of the blue, she'd been told her videos were boring.

She bit her lip, a knot of anxiety forming in her stomach. Her knees pulled up to her chest. "Do you think... maybe they're right? I mean, I've always been kind of shy on camera, maybe that's why they don't like it."

Max looked to his friend with a frown. There was criticism, and then there was this. He shook his head. "No. That's just trolling. It doesn't help us get better. They're just being mean."

She grimaced. "You have to say that."

He shook his head more firmly this time. "No, I really don't. If there's something you need to fix, I'll tell you. Like, remember when we tried that new intro, and I said it felt too stiff? That's the kind of thing I'd call out. But this? This is just trying to bring you down for no reason."

Max glanced back at the screen. "Trolls love to get a reaction. When they're vague and nasty like this, it's a dead giveaway."

She still looked anxious. "I don't know..."

Max's face scrunched up. He searched for the right words to explain. "It's like this. You know how I like to play Minecraft, and you can do whatever you want when you're playing it? Some people like to build stuff, some people hunt Endermen?"

Mei nodded tentatively.

"Well, think of Minecraft like YouTube, and your videos are

each a cool building you've made for your viewers. They can walk through it, check it out, enjoy it for what it is. Trolls though? They're not builders or even explorers. They just like to blow things up for fun. They're not there to appreciate your work— they're there to wreck it because they think it's funny."

Mei cracked a small smile. "So... they're like the creepers?"

"Exactly," Max said, grinning. "You're building for the players who want to be there, not the ones who sneak in to blow things up. Trolls are just creepers—don't let them destroy what you've built."

Hesitantly, Mei continued scrolling. A little further down, another comment caught her eye.

"Great video, but maybe you could explain the makeup steps a little more clearly. I got lost halfway through the contouring."

She pointed to it. "Okay, so is this trolling or constructive? I can't tell anymore."

Max read it over. "That one's actually helpful. See, they're not being mean—they're pointing out something we can fix. It's specific."

Mei nodded slowly, her brow furrowing in thought. "So, if they're just being vague and nasty, that's trolling?"

"Exactly," Max said, sitting up straighter. "Trolls want to tear us down, but constructive feedback is about helping us improve." He grinned. "We're making videos for people who actually care about what we're doing. If they're just telling us we suck, we can ignore them—they weren't our audience to begin with."

Mei smirked. "Like you said, they're the creepers of YouTube."

"Yeah, exactly," Max laughed. "Just waiting to blow up your build for fun."

Mei raised an imaginary hammer. "Time to grab the banhammer, then. No creepers allowed in our world."

Max grinned. "Now you're talking. Engaging with trolls only gives them power. The absolute best thing you can do to get back at trolls is to block them. It spoils their fun and takes away their game."

Mei did just that, feeling a rush of satisfaction as she hid the user from her channel. Then, feeling more confident, Mei pulled out her notebook and started jotting down ideas for her next video. As the comments rolled in, Max and Mei made a pact to filter out the noise, focusing on the voices that mattered—those who were supporting and helping them get better.

39
CRITIQUE HAPPENS

Respond gracefully to constructive feedback

Half an hour later, Max and Mei were both still working on their videos. They often did their filming independently – it just made more sense – but liked to get together to edit and brainstorm.

Mei's house had the biggest workstation, so they were both currently set up the desk in her bedroom – with the door open, of course. Mei's mom was still convinced the two were dating, which Mei found mortifying and Max hilarious.

Mei let out an annoyed huff.

"More trolls?" asked Max, glancing over.

Mei shook her head. "No, this one's... actually helpful," she sighed.

Pointing at the comment, she read it out to him. "I like the tutorial, but the steps for contouring were hard to follow. Could you slow down a bit and explain it better next time?"

Max leaned back; eyebrow raised. "Well, that's not so bad."

"It's not," Mei agreed, but she frowned slightly, biting the inside of her cheek. "But it still stings, you know? I worked really hard on that tutorial, and I thought it was pretty clear."

Max grabbed a Pringle from its can, crunching thoughtfully. "Yeah, I get that," he said eventually. "But it's not like they're saying you're bad at makeup. They're just asking for more detail."

Mei rolled her eyes. "Yeah, I know," she said. It was obvious she was still annoyed.

"Think of it this way," said Max. "You know how your mum watches those boring daytime soaps sometimes?"

"Yeah? What's that got to do with anything?".

"Would you ever write in and ask them to be more interesting?"

"Of course not!"

"Why not?"

Mei scrunched up her face. "They're not my thing. I don't care if they're boring – I was never going to watch them any...." She paused. "Ooh."

Max just raised an eyebrow.

"I think I see!" she exclaimed. "I'd only ever do that for stuff I really care about!"

Max grinned, glad she'd made the connection. "So... for this person to ask you to slow down and explain it better..."

"Yeah, yeah," Mei said. "You've made your point. They obviously care about my videos." Her face fell. "It's just... I guess I didn't expect feedback to hurt, even when it's useful."

"That's because we care about what we're doing," Max said,

voice soft. "It's normal to feel bummed when someone points out what we could do better. But that's how we grow, right?"

Mei nodded slowly, brow furrowed in thought. "Yeah. I guess I should thank them, huh? I mean, they're right. If I slow down and explain things more clearly, it'll make my videos better."

"Exactly!" Max grinned. "And who knows? Maybe this person will become a fan because you actually listened to their feedback."

Mei pulled up the reply box and started typing, her fingers moving a little slower than usual. "Okay. Here goes."

As she hit send, Max leaned back with a smile. "See? That's how you handle feedback like a pro."

Mei chuckled, feeling lighter. "It still stings, but yeah, I think I'm starting to get it. Turn critique into an opportunity."

Max nodded, then stretched his arms over his head with a grin. "Speaking of getting out... Kaia just texted. The girls are at the graffiti park. Said something about needing a creative release after a rough week."

Mei raised an eyebrow. "They okay?"

"I think so. Just sounds like they're dealing with haters too."

Mei grimaced. "We should be there for them."

Max grabbed his jacket. "Agreed. And honestly, a little spray paint therapy sounds like exactly what we need right now."

Mei smiled, pushing her chair back. "Let's go."

40
WAVING OFF THE HATERS

Leveraging support systems
Maintaining positivity

The graffiti park was as colorful as ever. Walls, benches, even the ground were covered in layers of artwork from different artists, each piece clashing and complementing the next in a chaotic but beautiful way. The surfer girls were deep in their work, cans of spray paint in hand.

The mural was already impressive—Kaia had outlined a huge wave crashing against the shore, with Lani adding colorful swirls to represent the spray. Piper had started painting a surfer riding the wave, her style bold and energetic.

"Glad you guys could make it," Kaia said, giving Mei a one-armed hug. "It's been one of those weeks."

Max grabbed a can, grinning as he surveyed their work. "Looks awesome," he said, shaking his can. "Mind if I add something?"

Kaia grinned. "Go for it. We need another surfer on that far wave. Think you could do something?"

Borrowing the long, straight edge from a cardboard box, Max stepped forward. The girls paused, curious, as he outlined a blocky shape by spraying short, sharp bursts of paint against the card, moving it after each one until he had a pixelated video game character on an equally blocky board, arms outstretched.

Standing so close to the wall, Max had accidentally angled the surfer on a diagonal, making it look like they were falling forward. "It's Gamer Steve, mastering the art of... face-planting," he laughed, once he finally noticed.

Mei surveyed her section of the wall. "Okay, I need to get in on this." She grabbed a bright pink can. With a quick sprays and liberal use of a black marker pen, she added a small figure next to Piper's surfer with exaggerated cat-eye makeup. "Glam Surfer Barbie," she said, stepping back to admire her work. "She never hits the beach without waterproof eyeliner."

The girls burst out laughing. "This is turning into the weirdest wave ever," Lani said, shaking her head with a grin. "But I love it."

As they continued painting, the conversation Kaia's day. "Somone gave me crap about my upcycling business today. Like, I shouldn't be allowed to take other people's junk and sell it at a profit. It's not fair, or something."

Mei frowned. "That's ridiculous. You literally find things on the side of the road. People are throwing them away!"

Kaia threw up her hands. "I know, right! I'm recycling stuff that would go to the dump. And it's a lot of work! I sand everything down, fix all the broken bits, stain it, paint it," she said, ticking things off on her fingers. "I'm basically building it from scratch!"

She shrugged. "It used to bother me more, but I've learned to tune it out. What matters is that I love what I do." She glanced at her friends. "And, I've got people who have my back."

Max nodded, stepping back from his part of the mural. "Yeah, we were just talking about that. Trolls and negativity suck, but when you've got a crew, it's easier to let it roll off."

Piper sprayed the finishing touches on her surfer, adding a streak of bright orange to the board. "You've just gotta focus on what you love, not what they hate."

The mural was nearly finished, a chaotic mix of surf, glitter, and video game characters, but the message was clear: it was a celebration of who they were. Not what others wanted them to be.

As they put away their cans, Mei felt lighter. The bad comments from this morning still stung, but they were starting to fade in the face of the laughter and camaraderie.

"You know what," Max said, stepping back with a grin. "This... was the best kind of therapy."

Mei nodded, a satisfied smile on her face. "Totally. Next time someone tries to knock us down, we'll just picture them face-planting like your gamer dude."

Max laughed. "Deal."

41
SPRAY SAFE OUT THERE!

Protecting personal information

Max adjusted the tripod, framing Mei perfectly for her livestream. The graffiti park looked vibrant behind her, a perfect backdrop for today's live session. Mei had ducked back to get her equipment and now had a microphone clipped to her shirt. Max was monitoring comments as behind-the-scenes tech support.

"Okay, we're live," Max said, giving her a thumbs-up.

Mei smiled into the camera, her hand holding a can of neon pink spray paint. "Hey everyone! Today, we're doing something a little different. I'm going to show you how street art is kinda like makeup—layering, blending, and adding details to make it pop." She gestured toward the wall behind her, where she had started outlining a design.

Max kept an eye on the chat as Mei went to work, narrating her steps. "You always want to start with a good base," she explained, spraying smooth strokes across the wall. "Just like foundation, it sets the stage for everything else."

The comments started rolling in, mostly positive. Max grinned - people were enjoying Mei's unique take on street art.

"Looking good!" he called out, reading a comment. "Someone says they love the color palette."

Mei laughed. "Thanks! I'm going for bold but blendable. Kinda like neon eyeliner."

Suddenly, a new comment popped up. Max frowned at the screen. "Uh, Mei... someone's asking for our location. They want to drop by and see the mural in person."

Mei paused mid-spray, glancing over at Max with a raised eyebrow. "Really? That's kinda cool..."

Max motioned for Mei to continue spraying. When her back was to the camera, he muted the microphone. "Okay, mic's muted. Let's take a minute to think this out before replying."

"Okay, what's up?"

"It just... feels a bit weird. Remember what Starlight Riot said? Don't ever tell viewers stuff that lets them find you in real-life. You need to protect your privacy."

Mei shrugged, keeping her back to the camera and her hand moving, so the audience wouldn't notice their conversation. "I mean, it's probably just a fan, right? Harmless."

Before Mei could reply, Kaia walked over from the other side of the park, holding her own can of paint. "No way," she said firmly. "Remember what happened with that creep at the cafe? We had to change our surf spot just to avoid him."

Half turning, Mei's eyes widened before she spun back to the wall, continuing to paint. "Whoa, I didn't know that."

Off camera, Kaia nodded seriously. "Yeah, it was a stressful couple of days. Almost got the police involved. Once he worked out where we surfed, he wouldn't leave us alone. Giving out your location is never a good idea. Even after the fact!"

Mei crinkled her nose. "But I'd be gone by then. What's the harm?"

"It's like leaving a trail of breadcrumbs," said Kaia. "They hear the name of this park in one video, then in another, you casually mention your favorite beach nearby. Before you know it, they've pieced together where you hang out. A few months later, some creepy dude is knocking on your door with flowers."

Mei paled. Taking several deep breaths, she motioned for Max to turn the microphone back on. Forcing cheerfulness, she turned and smiled at the camera. "I'm so honored that someone wants to come meet me in person!" she said, keeping her tone light. "But for safety reasons, I can't share my location while we're live. Gotta stay smart and safe out here!"

Mei glanced over at Max, who gave her a thumbs-up. She turned back to the mural, continuing to spray with a little more energy, the weight of the situation slowly lifting.

42
GROWING PAINS, GROWING GAINS

Growing through criticism
Think before you post!

Max and Mei wrapped up their session at the graffiti park as the last rays of sun dipped below the horizon. The sky was streaked with deep oranges and purples, casting a soft glow over their mural, which seemed to shimmer in the fading light. The wave they'd painted almost came alive, the vibrant colors catching the golden hues of dusk, with Mei's makeup-inspired swirls and Max's pixelated surfer character adding their own unique touch.

"Early morning surf tomorrow?" Kaia asked hopefully.

Max, about to say yes, hesitated, glancing at Mei. With a grimace, he shook his head. "Sorry. Would love to. But I think we should work on our channels. There are a couple of clips I need to edit to remove personal info from my last vid. Better be safe than sorry, you know?"

The girls nodded, remembering creepy guy. "Do what you gotta do to stay safe!" Kaia said. "See you round?"

Mei smiled, "Like a circle."

The following morning, the two met up at Max's house, laptops out, going over their recent videos with a more critical eye. They both scrolled through their content, pruning anything that gave away too much personal information. Max caught a clip where his street sign had flashed briefly in the background of his video, while Mei noticed a quick shot of her favorite café—too much of a breadcrumb for comfort.

"Okay, that's better," Mei said, clicking save.

Max nodded. They'd definitely learned their lesson.

With their videos now a little safer, they turned their attention to implementing the other feedback they'd received. Based on viewer comments, Max tweaked the pacing of his gameplay, slowing down his explanations to give new players more time to absorb the information. Mei refined her step-by-step makeup instructions, adding close-up shots to make each move clearer.

A week later, they found themselves once more at Max's house, both staring at his laptop in stunned silence.

"Okay, I didn't expect this," Max said, breaking the quiet.

Mei leaned in closer, her mouth hanging open. "Me neither."

Max's latest video, the one he'd edited based on viewer feedback, was doing far better than either of them had anticipated. Its view count was the best of any of his videos, and had singlehandedly added several hundred subscribers to his channel.

The comments were flooding in—this time positive.

Dude, your new pacing is perfect. I finally get
what you're saying, thanks!

Love the close-ups! Super helpful!

Max scrolled down, reading through everything. "I mean, I just slowed it down a bit and added those extra steps, but... look at the engagement. People are actually sticking around until the end now!"

Mei grinned. "It's because you listened. You took their feedback and made it better. That's how you grow."

Max leaned back in his chair, still in disbelief. "I guess so. It's crazy how a few changes can make such a big difference."

Mei nodded. "It's not just about making videos anymore, is it? It's about improving with each one, listening to the people who actually care."

Max smirked. "Yeah, and ignoring the creepers."

They both laughed. This... thing they had started was actually working! It wasn't the insta fame they'd both hoped for at the start, but with hard work and lessons learned, the numbers showed there was now a future for their dreams.

MEI'S NOTES:
HANDLING CRITICISM AND TROLLS

Constructive criticism helps you grow

Not all negative feedback is bad. Some comments, like suggestions on how to improve tutorials or pacing, can really help take your content to the next level.

Trolls are just creepers

Trolls exist to tear you down, not help you improve. The best thing to do is block them and move on - don't give them the power to ruin your creativity. *Repeat after me, they're not your audience Mei, they're not your audience.*

Protect personal info

After realizing how much personal information we were accidentally giving away, we cleaned up our videos to ensure our safety. No live locations, no breadcrumbs!

Listen to your audience

When we listened to helpful feedback, engagement and watch time improved. It's not about just making videos; it's about listening to the people who actually care about what you're creating.

Don't forget your support system

Whether it's the girls at the graffiti park or each other, having people who understand and support you makes handling negativity a lot easier.

Take care of yourself

Spray painting and laughing with friends was the best therapy after dealing with trolls. Remember to take breaks and do what makes you happy when things get tough!

Reminder

Max's "Gamer Steve" surfer is officially a masterpiece of modern art. Next time he suggests we "add something," I'm bringing a spare can of paint and lower expectations.

PART 9: COLLABORATION AND NETWORKING

In which our intrepid heroes discover that collaboration isn't just about juggling ideas—it's about catching each other's pins. Also, churros with ice cream are the true MVP.

43
THE JUGGLING DUO

The power of collaboration
Support others

Max and Mei spent the next week diving back into their YouTube channels, excited to see their hard work slowly paying off. They filmed a couple of fun videos—nothing groundbreaking, just stuff they genuinely enjoyed making. Max did a gaming tutorial while Mei played with a bold makeup look inspired by Pikachu, her favorite Pokémon character. It was fun, and they were loving the slow and steady growth.

That's why, when Max spotted a flyer for a Street Performer Festival, he immediately sent it to Mei.

We need to check this out! Might give us some fresh ideas for collabs. Max

Though Mei was skeptical, the promise of churros and live music won her over. Now, as they wandered through the festival, the streets buzzed with energy. The air smelled of kettle corn, and lively tunes from nearby performers filled the space.

"This place is pretty cool," Mei admitted, her eyes scanning the crowd. "Way more happening than I thought."

Max grinned. "Told ya."

The variety of performers was overwhelming. Making their way through the festival, they stumbled on a small stage where two performers—a juggler and a magician—were setting up. The juggler threw a practice pins into the air as the magician shuffled cards, both exchanging casual banter with the growing crowd.

"They're performing together?" Mei asked, eyebrow rising.

Max nodded. "Looks like it. That's kinda cool."

The act began with the juggler tossing pins into the air, but just when the crowd thought they were watching a standard juggling routine, the magician jumped in, producing a new pin out of thin air to add it to the mix. The crowd gasped as the two performers seamlessly worked together, blending their skills into one impressive routine.

Every so often, the magician paused to make a coin disappear, only to have the juggler "find" it again on one of the pins. The two bounced off each other, their chemistry clear as they kept the audience entertained. Their routine wasn't just about juggling or magic—it was about how they made it all work together.

At one point, the juggler even tossed a pin high into the air, and the magician caught it with a flourish before seamlessly launching into his next trick. The crowd loved it.

As they wrapped up their act, the magician gestured toward the nearby stage. "Make sure to check out the sword swallower down by the fountain! He's incredible!"

The crowd applauded as the performers took their bow, a huge chunk peeling off to investigate the sword performer as directed. Over their heads, Mei noted the suddenly swamped act waving his swords at the magician gratefully.

"That was really cool of them," commented Max. "They didn't have to give him a plug."

Mei nodded as they strolled through the festival, still buzzing from the energy of the performance. "I guess people don't just watch one performer, do they? Supporting other creators doesn't mean they're losing their own audience. Viewers don't have to go home after the first performer."

Max laughed. "I'd go nuts if I was only allowed to watch one!" He scratched his chin. "Actually, there's so many performers here, I'm kinda grateful to these guys pointing something else out!"

Mei frowned. "I hope the sword swallower lives up to the rec."

In the distance, a huge burst of flames rose into the air, followed by *oohs* and *ahhs* from the crowd.

"Guess that answers that question," Max laughed. "Wanna check them out?"

Mei hesitated. "Maybe later? It's kinda crowded."

Music floated to them from their right. They headed in that direction to see what they could find.

44
JAM SESSION

Building genuine relationships
Cross-promotion

Max and Mei wove through crowded streets until the music became clearer—acoustic guitars strumming, a violin weaving through the air, and someone keeping rhythm on a cajón box drum. It was a small circle of street musicians, casually jamming as a growing crowd gathered around them. Max and Mei slid into the group, watching as one of the guitarists flashed a grin and nodded toward a newcomer, a woman with a trumpet slung over her shoulder. Without hesitation, she jumped in, weaving brass notes into the melody as if they'd been playing together for years.

Mei grinned as the musicians played off each other naturally. "They're just... vibing," she said under her breath, as if not to disturb the flow.

Max nodded, transfixed. "Each one adds something different, but together it's like magic."

The guitarist, a guy with a pho-hawk and rolled up sleeves, stepped forward during a break between songs. "Hey folks, we're just a bunch of musicians hanging out. If you like what you're hearing, make sure to check out Jimmy on trumpet—she's got a gig at the café next weekend."

Jimmy grinned and added, "And don't miss our violinist at the market tomorrow. He's always cooking up something special."

Max noticed the audience giving appreciative nods. The crowd were now invested in all of them, thanks to how naturally they promoted each other.

The band kicked into another tune, blending folk and blues with a playful twist that had everyone swaying. Mei caught Max's eye and grinned, caught up in the easy back-and-forth energy of the group. There was something about it that was... inspiring. It was like, each musician was talented on their own, but together, they made something even bigger.

And though there was a hat out the front, Max got the feeling they'd be doing this even if there wasn't. This wasn't about the money, though he was sure that helped. The musicians seemed to enjoy every note. They shared smiles and lifted each other up.

The audience could tell it too. After the final note faded into the air, the crowd erupted into applause. Max and Mei looked at each other, then fished in their pockets for notes, adding them to the quickly filling hat.

45
CHEMISTRY FAIL

Dealing with challenges in collaboration
Finding the right partners

Max and Mei wove through the bustling festival. The sounds of the street performers, who had started up again, slowly faded as they moved through the throng of people. Laughter, applause, and the occasional cheer filled the air as they passed various performers, until they turned a corner, spotting a crowd gathering near a small outdoor stage. Two performers were about to start a show—a magician in a glittering purple cloak and a scientist in a white lab coat.

"Let's check it out," Max suggested, nudging Mei. The last duo they'd seen had been awesome, so he had high hopes for this one too. They slipped into the audience.

The magician began with a grand flourish, pulling a colorful silk scarf from an empty box, much to the audience's delight. She moved smoothly, her tricks well-practiced and polished, setting an enchanting tone.

Just as the audience was clapping, the scientist, standing next to a table filled with beakers and gadgets, stepped forward with a grin. "That's pretty cool, but let's see what happens when you mix baking soda and vinegar!" They quickly poured the two ingredients into a beaker, creating a bubbly volcano that fizzled over the sides.

The magician kept her smile, but it was clear from the way she hesitated that the timing of the science experiment had thrown her off. She moved on to her next trick, producing a dove from her sleeve with a flourish, only for the scientist to jump in once again. "No doves here, but I've got a reaction that flies just as high!" they said, tossing Mentos into a bottle of soda, causing a geyser of fizz to erupt into the air.

The audience laughed and cheered, but Max and Mei exchanged a glance. It was like watching two shows happening at once—both impressive, but completely different vibes. The magician's tricks were about mystery and illusion, while the scientist was all about tangible, cause-and-effect reactions.

As the performance went on, the magician subtly adjusted her pacing, trying to align with the scientist's slower, methodical style. She adapted her transitions, cutting down on the longer dramatic pauses, and instead, gracefully handed over moments for the scientist to explain the science behind the "magic." It was clear she was trying to make it work, even though the styles clashed. But the tension was obvious.

She set up a coin vanishing act, preparing to wow the crowd

with her sleight of hand. Just as the coin disappeared, the scientist leaned in, holding up a test tube filled with colored liquid. "Speaking of disappearing, let's watch this chemical reaction change color!"

The audience was caught between applause and chuckles, unsure of whether to be amazed or entertained. The performers were good—great, even—but their act felt like the scientist was trying to show up the magician, instead of working with her.

As the act wound down, the performers took a bow, though the applause felt more scattered than enthusiastic. The magician's smile was tight, and the scientist gave a half-shrug, as if to say, "It was fun while it lasted."

After the show, Max and Mei wandered toward the side of the stage where the magician was packing up her props. She gave them a tired smile as they approached.

"Hey, great show!" Mei said, trying to lift the mood.

The magician laughed lightly, brushing back her hair. "Thanks. I just wish it had gone smoother."

Max tilted his head. "You were awesome! But, uh... it seemed like your styles didn't quite match?"

The magician sighed, glancing over at the scientist. "Yeah, we're both good at what we do, but I guess I didn't think about how different our approaches are. I teamed up because she has a big following, but... we just don't gel. It felt like we were competing instead of collaborating."

Max raised an eyebrow. "So... what happens now?"

The magician smiled, a hint of relief in her voice. "We've agreed to part ways after this show. It's nothing personal—sometimes collaborations just don't work out, and that's okay. It's better to move on professionally than to keep forcing something that doesn't feel right, you know?"

Max and Mei grimaced in agreement. Definitely — as they'd seen in the street jam, when people clicked, it was amazing. But when they didn't? Well, you got... this.

46
A PERFECT MATCH?

Effective communication
Respect for boundaries

Max and Mei strolled away from the last show, disappointment about the magician-scientist debacle still hanging in the air. Mei sighed, glancing around at the bustling festival. "Well, that was… awkward."

Max shoved his hands into his pockets, brow furrowed. "Yeah. Total mood killer."

Without a word, Mei steered them toward a churro stand nearby. "Let's fix that," she said. After grabbing a churro, she turned to the ice cream stand next door. Max raised an eyebrow as she scooped up a small bowl of soft serve. Then, with a cheeky grin, she dunked the churro into the ice cream and held it up triumphantly like a prize. "You're welcome," she said, handing him the edible masterpiece.

Max blinked, then took a bite, his eyes widening. "Why have I never thought of this?" he mumbled through a mouthful of churro and ice cream. "This is… genius."

Mei chuckled, clearly pleased with herself.

They meandered back through the festival, Mei guiding Max—who was still marveling at his churro-spoon—to a crowd that had formed near the wall of one of the permanent buildings that the festival was built against.

A large space had been cleared, and two artists were in the process of painting an enormous mural. One of the artists, a guy in a wheelchair, seemed to be handling the lower section of the wall. Holding a spray can and dressed in splattered overalls, his hands moved with swift precision over the concrete. His section was gritty cyberpunk—neon signs, crumbling futuristic buildings, and wires snaking through dark alleyways. The harsh, bold colors gave the bottom half a chaotic energy.

Working above and around him, a woman with paintbrushes tucked into her hair was continuing his work in a totally different style. Using careful brush strokes and soft, dreamy pastels, she transformed each building into elegant spires and floating castles. Her fantasy city, glowing with magic and clouds swirling around it, contrasted beautifully with the roughness below.

In the middle, the two styles collided in a mesmerizing blend. Vines, shimmering with an otherworldly glow, crept up the neon-lit skyscrapers, while digital code seemed to leak from the enchanted towers, blurring the lines between the gritty city below and the magical realm above. The fusion of their styles was seamless, creating a world where fantasy and technology coexisted in perfect, surreal harmony.

"What are they doing?" Mei asked, fascinated.

"They're collaborating," Max breathed.

One of the artists overheard them and smiled. "We wanted to create something that brought together our strengths—urban energy and natural beauty," said the man in the wheelchair. "We talked a lot before starting, making sure we both knew what we wanted from the mural."

The woman, still blending her sunset, chimed in. "I think it's working, don't you?"

Mei nodded vigorously. "This is stunning! I *wish* I could paint like this. Such a cool fusion of styles."

The artists chuckled. "Thanks!" said the woman. "Yeah, we had to set some clear boundaries before we even picked up a brush. But it's paying off now."

Max tilted his head. "What kind of boundaries?"

"Well," she explained, "Rob here is all about big, bold statements. I like more detailed, delicate stuff. We had to figure out how our styles could mesh without one overpowering the other." She smiled as she glanced at her partner. "Turns out, if you respect each other's creative space, you can make something pretty cool together."

The graffiti artist nodded, his wheelchair rolling smoothly as he worked on another part of the wall. "We didn't want to clash or mess with each other's vision, so we talked it through, made sure we communicated what we each wanted, and figured out how to bring it together." He nodded to a large sheet of paper laying on a table nearby. "Didn't hurt to work out what we were going to do in advance, either."

Walking over, Mei realized the paper was actually a smaller version of what they were painting on the wall—effectively, a map they could both work from. She nodded thoughtfully. "I like that. You both get to keep your style, but it still feels like one big picture."

They watched as the artists continued to add to the mural, their different techniques blending seamlessly. The crowd around them murmured in appreciation as the mural grew, layer by layer, into something bigger and better than either of them could have done on their own.

Max took in the breadth of the mural, before glancing down to scoop more ice-cream with his churro. "The perfect collab," he sighed.

Mei chuckled. "Um, Max?"

"Yeah?"

"You talking about the street artists, or your meal?"

47
NETWORKING LIKE A NINJA

Giving credit
Networking

Max and Mei wandered through the festival as the last rays of sunlight dipped below the horizon. The twinkling lights flickered on, matching the buzz of excited voices weaving through the night air.

They stopped by the sword swallower's stage that they'd been eager to see earlier. Now, the performer stood at the center, his flaming swords casting golden reflections across the crowd. With a final flourish, he swallowed one effortlessly, earning gasps and cheers. He bowed deeply, then stepped forward with a grin.

"If you've enjoyed tonight's performances, I've got one more favor to ask—but it's not for me." He pointed toward the crowd, his voice warm and enthusiastic. "The magician and juggler duo you saw earlier are going for a Netflix special. Check out their Kickstarter if you're interested—they'd love your support!"

As applause rippled through the audience, he gestured toward a distant stage. "And now, for the grand finale. Head over to the main stage. Trust me, you don't want to miss this!"

The crowd buzzed with anticipation as people streamed toward the main stage. Max nudged Mei. "That was cool of him to hype up the magician. Especially since they gave him a shout-out earlier with no strings attached."

Mei tilted her head thoughtfully. "I guess when you help others, it kinda comes back to you? Funny how they accidentally started a collaboration."

"Yeah," Max said, nodding. "It's not really karma. More like... when you're nice to people, they're more likely to return the favor."

The main stage came into view, simple but elevated enough for the growing crowd. A woman with a calm, commanding presence stepped up to the microphone. She wasn't flashy—her outfit was plain, her hair tied back—but her quiet confidence pulled everyone in.

"Welcome, everyone," she said warmly. "Before we close out tonight, I want to thank the incredible artists who made this festival what it is. Their creativity, passion, and collaboration brought us together. If you loved what you saw, follow their work, share it, and let them know!"

Cheers erupted as the audience clapped for the performers who had made the night magical.

"And now," she continued, a small smile curling her lips, "let me share one final piece to end the night."

Her voice softened as she launched into a spoken-word poem, weaving together moments from the festival into a vivid narrative. Her words carried images of resilience, creativity, and connection, turning the festival's chaos into a single, glowing memory.

I came for the churros, stayed for the show,
Watched a juggler drop pins but pick up the flow.
Sword swallowers and street art—this place is a dream,
Where neon lights flicker and energy beams.

Max and Mei stood at the edge of the crowd, completely drawn in. The poem wasn't just a performance; it felt like a warm thread pulling everyone together. When she finished, the applause was thunderous, not just for her, but for every artist who had made the night unforgettable.

As the event eased into a more relaxed vibe, artists mingled in the crowd, sharing ideas, swapping contact info, and laughing. The poet moved gracefully through the throng, chatting with groups, her words sparking connection wherever she went.

"Man," Max said, nudging Mei, "this is how it's done. Everyone's got each other's back."

They wandered through the lively conversations, catching snippets of future projects and collaboration ideas. The mural artists were chatting with a digital animator about blending styles for a new project. Musicians brainstormed ways to incorporate spoken word into their sets.

Max grinned. "You know, we've been doing this since day one—collaborating, swapping ideas, helping each other out. I just didn't realize it's a thing in every creative community."

Mei nodded, her gaze following the poet. "Yeah, it's like this whole festival is one big networking event. But it's not just about performing—it's about growing and seeing what happens when you work with others."

The poet was a master at it. She'd drift into conversations, listen intently, and then offer help, like connecting people with friends or mentioning their work on her website. She never asked for favors, but people seemed eager to promote her anyway.

Max watched in awe. "It's like… when you help people without expecting anything back, they want to help you even more. Maybe karma really *is* a thing."

Mei gave him a curious look. "What'd you say?"

"Nothing," Max said with a shrug, lips twitching into a smile. "So, what's next? Do we find someone else to collab with?"

Mei laughed. "Maybe. But first, churros. I think the van's about to close up."

Max grinned as they followed the delicious scent. Collaboration could wait—churros *always* came first.

MEI'S NOTES:
COLLABS AND NETWORKING

Collaboration is a two-way street
Viewers don't just watch one channel, and supporting others makes
both creators and viewers feel appreciated. It's not just about taking
- it's about giving back too. Like the magician and sword swallower -
shouting each other out kept the audience engaged without taking away
from their own acts.

Starting a collab can be simple
It's as easy as talking about the things you love, then reaching out
and letting that channel know what you've done (because it never
hurts to help them know who to be thankful for!).

Collaboration amplifies creativity
When two people bring different talents together, the results can be
magical - like the juggler and magician tossing pins and cards back and
forth. Sure, juggling and magic are cool separately, but together? That
was next-level awesome.

Find the right collaboration partner
Not every collab is going to work. Just because someone's popular doesn't mean your styles will mesh. The magician and scientist? Yikes. They were both great solo, but their act felt more like a competition than a team effort. Lesson learned: make sure you vibe before teaming up!

Communication is everything
The mural artists nailed this. They had a plan, clear boundaries, and a shared vision before they even picked up their brushes. That's why their cyberpunk-meets-fantasy city worked so well - everything blended seamlessly. Without communication, though? Total chaos.

It's okay if collaborations don't work out
Sometimes, no matter how much you try, a collab just won't click. Like the magician and scientist - they decided to part ways, and that's okay. It's better to move on than to keep forcing something that doesn't feel right.

Genuine relationships
When you truly connect with others, supporting each other's work happens naturally - just like the musicians who promoted each other's gigs without even trying.

Networking is about giving first

The poet was a master at this. She offered to help others without asking for anything back, and they wanted to help her in return. Building genuine relationships is key to long-lasting success - her network became a circle of friends, not just business partners. Note to self: start by asking, "How can I help?" instead of "What's in it for me?"

Kindness encourages reciprocity

Maybe karma *is* a thing. When you're kind and support others, they're way more likely to return the favor. The magician gave the sword swallower a shout-out, and he hyped her right back. It's not magic - it's just how people work.

Churros are life-changing

Pro tip: Never let Max near your churro-and-soft-serve combo. Show him the trick, and he'll claim it as his forever!

PART 10: MONETIZING YOUR CHANNEL

In which our intrepid heroes unlock the secrets of monetization, discover the hidden talents of Cuthbert Jr., and learn that churros taste even better when you've got a tote bag full of fresh ideas.

48
LEVELING UP IRL

Diversifying income streams

Things were finally looking up for Max and Mei. Over the past few months, they'd found their niches, pooled resources to buy decent equipment, and worked hard to create compelling content. Cumulatively, people had spent thousands of hours watching their videos!

With the basics sorted, they'd gone on to create strong brands, boost audience engagement, and format their videos to play nice with YouTube's algorithm.

Though nobody really knew what made YouTube tick, their efforts at consistency, quality, using keywords, improving thumbnails, and reminding people to *like, subscribe, and comment* were finally paying off.

Literally.

Max and Mei sat in Mei's bedroom, laptops open on her desk, each with a finger poised over their keyboards.

"Ready?" Mei asked, grinning nervously.

Max nodded. "Let's do this."

Together, they clicked "yes."

It was a small, insignificant movement, but it signified their biggest leap forward yet. They'd both just applied to monetize their YouTube videos, an action they'd feared nearly impossible when their journeys started not so long ago.

Monetizing on YouTube wasn't automatic. Max and Mei had made a lot of videos, and though ads ran on them, they hadn't seen a cent. Before earning anything, they had to prove their channels had real momentum—hitting milestones like a certain number of subscribers and hours watched. It was like proving you knew all the moves before stepping onto the main stage.

Now, with those clicks, they were officially stepping onto the dance floor.

They only made a few cents per ad, if that, and would need millions more subscribers to buy their parents a house or arrive at school in a private helicopter. But maybe—just maybe—that first paycheck would cover a celebratory churro.

"We should celebrate," Max said, shutting his laptop.

Mei smirked. "Churros?"

Max grabbed his jacket. "Absolutely churros."

The night air was cool as they walked through the busy streets, the glow of colorful market stalls lighting up the evening. It was the perfect mix of food, crafts, and an eclectic range of handmade items. The air smelled like sizzling meat, caramelized sugar, and roasted nuts. Mei's eyes were immediately drawn to a stall selling hand-painted tote bags, each one uniquely designed with vibrant colors and quirky illustrations.

"Whoa, check these out!" Mei exclaimed, pulling Max over.

The vendor, a woman with bright pink hair and round glasses, looked up from her work and smiled. "You like them? I hand-paint each one. These are my passion projects."

"They're amazing," Mei said, picking one with a neon rainbow cat. "Do you sell them online?"

"Yeah, I have an Etsy shop, plus I sell at markets like this. Oh, and I've recently started partnering with subscription box services to get them out there even more." She waved a hand toward her display. "Gotta diversify where you can, right?"

Max raised an eyebrow. "Diversify?"

The vendor nodded. "Yep. Selling online means I can keep earning even when I'm not here. Partnering with boxes gets my stuff in front of new customers. And markets let me meet people like you. If one stream slows down, the others keep me going. It's all about spreading the risk."

Max and Mei exchanged a thoughtful glance. Their end goal had always just been monetization, but wouldn't it be smarter to spread the risk out? Logan Paul sold energy drinks, and even Mr. Beast sold chocolate bars! If the YouTube greats were doing it, they should consider it too.

They nodded. Maybe not right away, but game-related stuff for

Max and makeup accessories for Mei totally made sense down the track.

Mei handed the tote back to the vendor with a smile. "Thanks for the tips—and the inspiration. What's your Etsy shop? I'll mention it in one of my videos."

The vendor beamed. "That'd be awesome! Here's my card."

As they walked away, Max nudged Mei. "So… churros?"

"Churros," Mei agreed.

The celebration wasn't fancy, but as they bit into the warm, sugary treats, the possibilities ahead of them felt endless.

49
SMART MONEY

Monetizing physical and digital products
Subscription revenue
Affiliate marketing

Max and Mei wove through the bustling night market, the twinkling lights and festive atmosphere pulling them in every direction. Stalls brimmed with quirky crafts, sizzling food, and clever gadgets, the air alive with laughter and music. But Max's focus was singular.

"Come on," he said, sniffing the air. "I smell churros."

Mei rolled her eyes but followed, pausing every so often to marvel at the displays. A vendor demonstrating LED wristbands caught her attention. "Max, look! They sync to the music! How cool is that?"

Max barely glanced over his shoulder. "Yeah, yeah, awesome. We can come back after chur—" He froze mid-sentence, eyes widening at a glowing booth ahead. "Wait. Is that... Cuthbert?"

Mei's jaw dropped. "No way! The peace lily from the tech fair?"

Pushing through the crowd, they found themselves face-to-face with *Cuthbert's Smart Pot Holders*. Although the stall was rather plain, the pots on display all had sleek designs. They glowed in soft hues, each housing a plant, including their old friend, Cuthbert the peace lily. Next to the pots was a small screen showing off a connected app.

"It's you two!" the inventor from the tech fair exclaimed, still sporting his trademark toolbelt. He waved them over enthusiastically. "I owe you big time. Putting me in touch with Cuthbert here was the missing piece. Look how far we've come!"

Cuthbert's owner smiled warmly, motioning to the pots. "We decided to partner up! These are our smart plant holders. They monitor soil moisture, light exposure, and more, all synced to an app. No more guesswork for plant care."

Whoa," Max said, leaning in. "So it's like... a Fitbit for plants?"

"Exactly!" the owner said with a laugh. "And the app's free. But for premium features—like custom care tips and reminders—we offer a subscription."

Mei nodded slowly, clearly impressed. "So the app hooks people in, but the subscription is how you really make money?"

"Bingo," the owner said. "Oh, and we're adding affiliate marketing soon. When someone's plant needs fertilizer, they can buy it directly through the app. We get a small cut for recommending trusted products."

Max and Mei exchanged thoughtful glances. Mei tapped her chin. "So, you're making money from the pots, the app, and partnerships? That's... really smart."

"We're trying," the owner said modestly. "Crazy Mike here—" he clapped the inventor on the shoulder, "—helped us refine the design to make the pots affordable. It's all about building trust first, then scaling up."

Max chuckled. "Cuthbert's becoming a plant celebrity."

"You have no idea," the owner said. "People send us pictures like they're proud parents."

"Wow. That's so cool," Max enthused. "What next? Will you scale up, try and take this big? It's a great idea."

"Honestly, right now we're just trying to build slowly," Cuthbert's owner said. "We'll probably put the money we make from sales tonight into jazzing up the stall a bit—you know, make it more interesting."

"Hmm," Max wiggled his nose, deep in thought, imagining vines growing up buildings.

"What are you thinking?" asked Mei.

"That graffiti artist from the street festival..." Max began.

"...could make an amazing backdrop here!" Mei finished.

Cuthbert's owner looked at them quizzically.

"We met this cool duo at a street festival last week," Max explained. "They were painting this huge mural. One dude did the bottom with this cool neon graffiti vibe, while another did the most stunning fine art piece on top. Their work would look absolutely awesome here, and I know they were looking for places to hang it. Maybe they could help you, if you helped them?"

Cuthbert's owner's eyes widened. "I'd be happy to put a price tag under their work!"

After receiving the artist's number, Cuthbert's owner thrust a potted plant into Max's hands. "Thank you so much. I know you didn't expect anything, but you've been so helpful. Just... thanks."

Bemused, Max and Mei continued their quest for the ultimate churro, this time accompanied by Cuthbert Jr.

50
A MERCH MADE IN HEAVEN

Sponsorship & merchandising

Max and Mei wandered through the bustling night market, Cuthbert Jr. nestled comfortably in Max's arms. The little plant seemed to have taken to the adventure, its leaves fluttering with every bounce. Strings of twinkling lights cast a warm glow over the eclectic stalls, and the air was alive with the hum of conversation, bursts of laughter, and the strum of a street guitarist. The scent of churros danced tantalizingly in the breeze.

"Where to next?" Max asked, readjusting Cuthbert Jr. as they strolled past a booth selling intricately carved wooden puzzles.

Mei spotted a banner in bold, graffiti-like lettering. Her eyes lit up. "Wait a sec... isn't that Starlight Riot?"

Max whipped around, his face breaking into a grin. "No way. It is!"

The stall was decked out in all things Starlight Riot: vibrant t-shirts, eye-catching posters, stickers, and tote bags that practically begged to be bought. It was a miniature shrine to the band they'd been obsessing over since sneaking into their concert.

Behind the table stood a woman with bright pink streaks in her hair, her shirt proudly displaying the band's logo. She spotted them gawking and smiled. "You kids fans?"

"The biggest," Mei said, stepping closer to run her fingers over a t-shirt's raised design. "These are amazing. The colors, the texture—it's perfect."

"Thanks!" the woman said proudly. "We work hard to get these right. It's all about capturing the band's energy, you know? Bold, authentic, a little rebellious. That's Starlight Riot."

Max picked up a tote bag featuring the lead singer mid-stage dive. "You work for the band?"

She laughed, shaking her head. "Not quite. But I do run the print shop that makes all their merch. We've been collaborating for a while now—it's been incredible."

Mei tilted her head. "Wait, so how does that work? You guys design all this together?"

"Yep, pretty much," the woman said, leaning against the table. "We handle all the production, but work closely with the band to nail their vibe. They trust us to keep it true to who they are. That's why it works."

Max raised an eyebrow, intrigued. "Doesn't all this cost a ton to make?"

"Normally, yeah," she said, tapping the corner of the table. "But it's a partnership. We cover the production costs upfront, and in return, the band gives us shout-outs at gigs, and our shop's logo goes on the back of every shirt. It's a win-win."

She flipped over a t-shirt to show them the logo, subtly placed under the design. "We get exposure to fans who love supporting indie artists, and the band gets merch without the huge financial burden. Plus, it keeps everything local and personal—just like the band."

"That's genius," Mei said, her eyes scanning the colorful display.

"It really is," Max added, holding up a sticker with the band's name in electric green. "It's not just about making stuff. It's about finding the right people to work with."

"Exactly," the woman said, her voice warm with enthusiasm. "When it clicks, it's magic. The fans know when something's real, and they appreciate that. If we tried to slap their name on, I don't know, some random dish soap, it wouldn't feel right. But because we share their love for local music and art, it works."

Mei picked up a poster, admiring the bold design. "Do you think they'd work with smaller creators?"

"Maybe," the vendor said thoughtfully. "You'd have to ask. But the point is, partnerships aren't just about money. It's about shared values, shared goals. The shop loves Starlight's music, and the band respects what the shop stands for. That's why it works."

Mei chuckled, holding up the poster. "One day, we'll have our own merch stand, and people will be lining up for *our* stuff."

The vendor winked. "I'll save a spot for you," she said.

Max and Mei thanked her before moving on through the bustling market. Max held Cuthbert Jr. up as they walked. "Think you'll get a sponsor soon too? You could be the first plant influencer."

Mei snorted, shaking her head. "He's got the look for it—those leaves are practically glowing. Just wait till he starts promoting premium plant food."

Max grinned. "This video is brought to you by Cuthbert Jr.—thriving on only the finest nutrients.'"

They both laughed. "He'll be bigger than both of us someday."

Max dipped the plant into a nod. "I just hope he remembers us when he's famous."

51
FUNKY BEATS AND FUNDING FEATS

Crowdfunding and tipping

Max, Mei, and Cuthbert Jr. were drawn to a crowd gathered on the sidewalk, captivated by a street dancer moving effortlessly to an upbeat, funky track. The dancer twirled, leaped, and popped with smooth precision, each movement synchronized to the rhythm. The music pulsed through the speakers, and the energy of the performance radiated outward, pulling more people in.

At the end of the routine, the dancer smiled, catching her breath as the audience erupted in applause. She bowed with a flourish and motioned towards a small sign with a QR code that read: "*Support my art - digital tips welcome!*" Max and Mei exchanged a glance, curious about the setup.

Max stepped forward, scanning the QR code. "Is this how you make most of your money?" he asked, giving the artist five dollars.

The dancer beamed. "Thanks!" she said. "Name's Lexie. Tips help, but my bread and butter is Patreon."

"Patreon?" Mei echoed, intrigued.

"Yeah, it's this platform where fans can subscribe monthly," Lexie explained. She adjusted her bright blue sneakers and gestured to her setup. "I post tutorials, behind-the-scenes clips— basically stuff you can't get anywhere else. It's like giving fans VIP access to your work."

Max tilted his head. "So, it's like a club for your audience?"

Lexie laughed. "Exactly! Like, my top tier gets to pick a song for me to choreograph. I mean, my fans chose this track," she said, pointing to her speaker. "And that Kickstarter sign over there? That's how I funded these speakers and this costume. People wanted to see me take my performances to the next level, so they helped make it happen."

Max watched as a group of teens scanned the QR code and tipped, chatting animatedly about Lexie's last move. She waved at them, thanking them between breaths.

"She makes it look so easy," Mei muttered, more to herself than anyone else.

"Hard work pays off," Lexie quipped, overhearing. She grabbed a bottle of water and continued. "I spend a lot of time talking to my audience, answering comments, and asking what they want to see. It's less about 'give me money' and more like inviting people to be part of the creative process."

Max nodded, watching as a little kid excitedly twirled in front of Lexie, mimicking her moves. Lexie grinned, spinning him around once before returning to the conversation.

Mei's gaze lingered on the kid. "I like that—it's not just about the money. It's about letting people feel like they're part of it."

"Exactly," Lexie agreed, tying her curly hair back. "When people feel included, they want to stick around—and maybe even help out. Like your channels! If you've got a dedicated audience, you can offer them something extra in return, something they'll actually love."

Max scratched his chin thoughtfully. "I guess we could do something like that too, maybe put some exclusive behind-the-scenes stuff or game tips on Patreon."

"You're gamers?" asked Lexie.

"Sort of? We have YouTube channels—mine's about gaming, Mei does cosplay tutorials."

Her eyes widened. "We totally have to talk," Lexie enthused. "I've got this video idea for a cool zombie dance, but I'm really struggling with the makeup."

Mei grinned. "Maybe a collab? I do your makeup, you let me film the process."

"Sounds great! I can feature your channel in the credits!"

"And I can have a link to your routine!"

The two exchanged numbers as Max held Cuthbert Jr. high. "Don't forget to credit him," he joked.

"Cuthbert Jr.'s the real star," Lexie said with a wink. "But seriously, you should think about Patreon. Let your audience vote on your next big idea, maybe run polls to keep them engaged. It's a game-changer."

Max raised his plant in agreement. "Cuthbert's ready to monetize. He's going to start offering premium oxygen packages."

Lexie doubled over laughing. "Okay, that's genius. You two are a riot. Hey, I've got another set to prep for, but if you're free later in the week, I'm organizing a flash mob event at the plaza. You should swing by!"

Mei clapped her hands. "A flash mob? Count us in."

MEI'S NOTES:
MONETIZING YOUR CHANNEL

Monetizing requires effort

It wasn't like we could just sit back, let ads run, and wait for the cash to roll in. Before earning anything, we needed to prove our channel had real momentum - reaching milestones like subscribers and watch hours. Basically, we had to show YouTube we knew all the dance moves before we were allowed on the main stage.

Diversify income streams

Relying on ad revenue is like putting all our coins in one piggy bank - risky. Instead, we need to spread things out. Ads, merch, sponsorships, even digital content - like the vendor with her hand-painted tote bags. It's about building a stable revenue stream, so if one source has a slow month, the others keep us afloat.

Hybrid monetization

Combining physical and digital products can create more opportunities. The smart pot holder's combination of an actual product and an app-based subscription is an excellent example of how to use both worlds to support a creative venture. Maybe Max could sell game guide books or something? Note to self: also investigate branding physical make-up products.

Crowdfunding and audience support
Platforms like Patreon let people build strong connections with their audience. Lexie, the street dancer, showed us that people genuinely want to support the creators they love. By giving fans exclusive content, tutorials, or just sharing good vibes, they're more likely to be part of our journey.

Sponsored content is all about fit
Sponsorships shouldn't feel awkward or forced. Finding sponsors that align with your content keeps things authentic. Nobody wants to see a gamer like Max pushing shampoo - it just doesn't add up.

Build relationships with your audience
Getting the audience involved is a win-win. We could put up exclusive content on Patreon or polls that let viewers decide our next video. When people feel like they're part of the journey, they're more likely to support us, both financially and emotionally.

Brand sponsorship = win-win

Sponsorship isn't just about the money; it's about finding partners who fit your vibe. Like Starlight Riot and that local print shop - it felt genuine, and they didn't have to foot the bill all on their own. Good sponsorships benefit both sides and feel like a natural fit. If I don't do my own makeup line, getting sponsored by a makeup company might be a good fit?

Collaboration can create opportunity

Lexie's zombie makeup collab idea was proof that a simple conversation can lead to something awesome. It's all about talking about what you love, offering your help, and letting those connections blossom. Collaboration helps everyone grow, and sometimes, it's as easy as sharing skills.

Cuthbert Jr

Apparently, carrying around a potted plant named Cuthbert Jr. makes you about 50% more approachable at a night market. Seriously, he might be our new secret weapon for sponsorships... "Plantfluencer" in the making?

PART 11: GOING VIRAL

In which our intrepid heroes stumble into the chaos of a flash mob, lose track of where the performance ends and the real world begins, and walk away with an idea they're sure could change everything.

52
START WITH A BANG

Trends and timing
The hook—first few seconds
The element of surprise

Max and Mei were bursting with excitement. Their YouTube channels were gaining traction, and while their earnings statements hadn't rolled in yet, it didn't matter. The real thrill came from watching their hard work pay off, knowing they were building something with lasting value.

"I mean, we're not making bank just yet," Max said, scrolling through the analytics on his phone. "But this feels more like a comet anyway, you know?"

Mei raised an eyebrow. "A comet?"

"Yeah! Like, we're not some flash-in-the-pan shooting star. We're the slow, steady kind of awesome. We're going to keep shining, not burn out."

Mei smiled, fingers dancing over her notebook. "I like that. Slow, steady, but still bright enough to make an impact."

They both knew their earnings would be small at first, but that wasn't the point. The focus was on creating quality content, and getting the basics right, trusting the rest would follow. As they put on their jackets and boarded a bus to Lexie's flash mob event, they joked that in the future, maybe they'd even earn enough for more than just churros at the local food truck!

"Fat chance," Max laughed, grabbing a strap as the bus pulled out. "If I had more money, I'd just buy the food truck!"

Excitement buzzed through the crowd as they disembarked at the square where Lexie had told them her flash mob would occur. It seemed their new friend had let more than just Max and Mei know what was happening!

"I hope this isn't some weird interpretive dance thing," Max muttered, glancing around the square.

Mei snorted. "You say that, but you'd totally join in."

"Only if I can floss," Max said with a grin.

While waiting, they noticed a street performer standing to one side. Imitating a statue, he was painted head to toe in gold, holding a plate before him.

"Bet you can't make him move," Max challenged.

Mei rolled her eyes but fished a coin from her pocket. "Fine." She stepped up to the statue and dropped a coin onto the plate.

What happened next, neither could have predicted.

The statue came to life with dramatic, robotic motion. Its limbs

jerked in time to an unseen rhythm, movements mechanical but full of energy. The busker marched to the center of the square, and as if on cue, music began to pulse through hidden speakers.

"Whoa..." Mei whispered, taking a step back.

One person in the crowd, a mother holding her toddler on her hip, caught Mei's eye. She seemed like any other bystander, watching the scene unfold with a gentle smile. But then, as if by some unseen signal, the mother started to sway. At first, it was subtle—just a casual shift of her weight as she rocked her child—but soon her movements became deliberate, flowing in perfect sync with the busker.

Mei blinked in surprise. "Is she... part of this?"

The woman, still holding her now giggling toddler, moved gracefully to the rhythm, her free arm lifting and twisting as if she'd rehearsed this moment for weeks. One by one, more seemingly ordinary people joined in—students, elderly couples, even a guy in a business suit—all dancing in perfect time. The surprise wasn't just that the flash mob had started, but that it could be anyone.

Before they knew it, Max and Mei were standing in the center of a fully choreographed group of dancers. People around them were moving in perfect time; it was impossible to tell who was part of the act, and who was just a stunned observer.

Max's jaw dropped.

"Lexie's good," Mei laughed, spinning around to take it all in.

The music, the dancing, the spontaneous energy — it was contagious.

But even as she twirled and laughed, Mei's mind was working. This was exactly the kind of thing she and Max needed to incorporate into their videos. The flash mob had started with an ordinary moment—a busker, a coin—but then something unexpected had turned it into a spectacle. That first surprising movement was the hook, the thing that grabbed everyone's attention and didn't let go.

"Max," she said, tugging on his sleeve as the mob danced around them, "this is what we need."

He raised an eyebrow, still swaying along. "A flash mob?"

"No," she shook her head. "The surprise. The hook. The busker just standing there, right? But then—bam! He moves, and then there's a mother, but she's not *just* a mother. And suddenly we're all in the middle of something incredible. That's what hooks people. We need to start our videos like this, with something unexpected right in the first few seconds."

Max's eyes widened as he caught on. "Like, show the punchline before the setup? Hit 'em with something that makes them stop scrolling?"

"Exactly," Mei nodded.

The crowd clapped as the music faded, and for a moment, it seemed like the flash mob had finished. People around them buzzed with excitement, some pulling out their phones to rewatch what had just unfolded. Max and Mei exchanged a glance, still processing what they'd been a part of.

"That was wild," Max said, catching his breath. "It was like we were inside the video for a minute."

Mei nodded, her mind still racing with ideas. "Yeah, and that hook—it was perfect. We need to do something like that."

Before they could dive deeper into planning their next video, the busker—now fully animated—took a slow, deliberate step toward them. He raised one arm in a grand gesture, and the music swelled again, louder this time. The crowd, including Max and Mei, turned as one, realizing the performance wasn't over.

"Wait—there's more?" Max asked, wide-eyed.

Mei's heart raced as a new wave of dancers stepped in, their moves synchronizing perfectly with the beat. The busker winked at Mei as if to say, "You're coming with us," and before they knew it, the flash mob wasn't just a spectacle—it was moving. Slowly at first, then gaining momentum, the dancers began flowing into the street, drawing curious onlookers into the performance as they went. The whole thing seemed to be spreading like wildfire, with more people joining as the dancers weaved through the streets.

Max laughed, his eyes wide with excitement. "If we had been five minutes late, we'd have missed the whole thing." He shook his head in disbelief, the energy of the crowd sweeping him along. "This is insane."

Mei grinned, feeling the buzz of the growing mob around her.

"Yeah, but we weren't late, were we?" she said, letting herself get pulled into the moving party. It was the kind of spontaneous moment that felt perfectly timed, even though no one had seen it coming.

Laughing and dancing, Max and Mei joined the mob as it flowed out into the streets.

53
RELATABLE RHYTHMS

Understand your audience
Emotional appeal
Keep it relatable

"It's turned into a full-on street party!" Max shouted over the music, his eyes wide with excitement.

The flash mob had transformed into something bigger—dancers, bystanders, and even curious onlookers were all moving together as one giant wave through the streets. Mei felt the rush of the moment, holding up her phone to capture it all.

But it wasn't just the movement that was catching her attention. As they wove through the crowd, she began to notice the little things. A dancer high-fived a young kid who was watching with his parents, sending the child into a fit of giggles. Another dancer handed a watching teen an invisible "microphone," prompting her to belt out an exaggerated, off-key note.

An elderly couple nearby smiled as a third dancer bowed graciously to the elderly lady, extending a hand with a playful flourish. She laughed, accepting the invitation, and the two began a slow, graceful waltz. The performer's movements were gentle and respectful, spinning her lightly before guiding her back toward her partner. With a wink, the performer then took the elderly man's hand, joining him with his wife in a quiet, joyful dance. Laughter rippled through the crowd, and people began clapping along, caught up in the moment.

Mei nudged Max. "Look at how everyone's reacting. It's not just about the dancing—they're connecting with everyone here."

Max nodded, filming it all on his phone. "Yeah, it's like... they're getting everyone to feel like they're part of it."

As they continued to move through the street, Mei could see how Lexie's troupe had planned the flash mob to appeal to a wide audience. There were families with kids, teenagers filming on their phones, and even older folks joining in. Each dancer was adding small, playful moments, but they weren't random. Mei could feel the emotional impact—everyone could relate to something.

The performers weren't just doing flashy moves; they were making people smile, laugh, and feel connected. A young girl in the crowd mimicked one of the dancers, and the dancer playfully copied her in return. The girl's face lit up, and Mei caught herself grinning.

"This is why it works," she said softly, more to herself than to Max. "It's not just about the moves. They're making it relatable... fun for everyone."

The small, human moments were what stuck. It wasn't about perfect choreography or flashy moves; it was about making everyone feel like they belonged in that moment.

As the crowd continued to dance and laugh, Mei caught a glimpse of Lexie at the head of the group, signaling the next phase of the flash mob. The dancers began to move faster, sweeping more people into the streets. The energy was contagious, and Mei could feel the shift.

"We better keep up," she said to Max, grabbing his arm. "This isn't over yet."

Max grinned, locking his phone to join the action. "Let's see where this takes us.

54
HASHTAG MOMENT

Create shareable content
Encourage engagement
Encourage sharing

The street pulsed with energy as the flash mob swept through, pulling everyone along with it. Max and Mei were caught up in the wave of excitement, laughing and recording the action on their phones. The dancers had drawn in families, teenagers, even elderly couples, turning the entire crowd into part of the performance.

"Come on, join in!" Lexie called out as she passed by, twirling a kid from the audience into a playful spin. The boy beamed, his face lighting up as he tried to mimic the dancers.

Before Max and Mei knew it, they were pulled into the circle, too. Mei hesitated for a second, but Max gave her a playful nudge. "You either dance, or film me looking ridiculous," he joked.

Mei laughed and joined in, copying a simple dance move another dancer showed them. The crowd around them clapped, cheered, and pulled out their phones to capture every moment.

The atmosphere was electric, full of laughter and spontaneity.

But then, slowly, the dancers started to disappear. It happened so gradually that Max and Mei didn't notice at first. People were still dancing and having fun, but something felt different. The crowd looking around in confusion. Where had the dancers gone?

Max frowned. "Are we... being ghosted?" The music quieted, and people stumbled to a stop, uncertain what was happening.

Then suddenly a cheer went up from the back. Mei turned to see it: the dancers hadn't vanished—they had reappeared, high above on a nearby rooftop. Lexie stood front and center, leading them in a final, synchronized routine. From their elevated position, they looked like performers on a grand stage, silhouetted against the sky.

The crowd erupted into applause and cheers, phones snapping up to capture the breathtaking finale. Max grinned, raising his phone to get the perfect shot. "That's how you end a show."

As the music faded, Lexie called out, "Don't forget to post your videos! Use the hashtag *#FlashRiot* and let's see how far we can spread this!"

Max and Mei exchanged a look. They could already see the hashtags trending, the videos going viral. This was more than just a fun experience—it was shareable, memorable, something people would talk about and send to their friends.

Pulling her book from her pocket, she started scribbling notes.

55
RUN WITH IT

Don't be afraid of experimentation
Collaboration can expand reach
Consistency and quality

Max and Mei leaned against the railing, catching their breath as the last few dancers made their way down from the rooftop. The energy from the flash mob still crackled in the air, leaving the crowd buzzing with excitement.

Lexie sauntered over, wiping sweat from her brow, a wide grin plastered on her face. "What'd you think?"

"That was insane," Max said, still a little breathless. "You pulled in everyone—from that mom with her kid to the guy in the business suit. How do you even plan something like that?"

Lexie chuckled, glancing back at the dispersing crowd. "Honestly? Some of it you plan, and some of it you just let happen. We had the core routines down, but the magic? That was collaboration," she said. "I couldn't have done this alone. I brought in dancers from different styles—hip-hop, contemporary, even that street performer we ran into a few weeks ago. Not only did they help build something bigger, but they helped spread the word as well."

Mei pointed back at the waltzing couple who were still laughing and twirling in the square. "You didn't plan for them to join though, did you?"

"Not at all!" Lexie beamed. "That fell into the *just let it happen* category. We saw them having a good time, so one of the dancers brought them in. It's those spontaneous moments that people remember. They feel like they're part of something bigger."

Max leaned on the railing, his mind racing. "So, how do you prep for that? I mean, you can't predict it, but you still made it work."

Lexie wiped her brow and leaned against the railing next to them. "You have to be ready for the unexpected. We rehearsed the basics until it was second nature. That way, when things go off-script—like the rooftop bit—we're ready to adapt. You saw how we threw that in when the crowd was starting to fade, right? We just read the vibe and switched it up."

Behind them, one of the dancers flipped over a trash can and used it as a makeshift drum, gathering a crowd of onlookers. Lexie gestured. "See that? Give them something different, something unexpected, and they're hooked. That's what makes it shareable."

Mei scribbled a note in her book. "So it's like... you lay the groundwork, but leave room for the audience to fill in the rest?"

"Exactly!" Lexie said, nodding. "People love to feel involved. The more they feel like they're part of the experience, the more they'll want to share it. It's not just about performing for them; it's about pulling them in."

Max watched as the crowd slowly thinned out. "And the surprise elements? That rooftop bit—nobody saw that coming."

Lexie grinned. "That's the hook. You need that moment where everyone's like, 'Wait, what just happened?' It doesn't have to be huge, but it has to make people stop and pay attention. Surprise them, keep them guessing. That's what gets people talking."

Max nudged Mei with his elbow. "We need something like that for our next video. Something quick, something that makes people feel like they're in on it."

Lexie clapped them both on the shoulders. "You guys already have the right idea. Just make sure you've got the basics nailed down first, then let the rest flow. Be ready for anything, and if luck shows up? Run with it."

56
READY, SET...

Short and impactful
Storytelling is key
Luck plays a role

Max and Mei burst into the living room, still riding the high from the flash mob. Jackets half off, they flopped onto the couch, breathless but buzzing with energy.

"I can't sit still. We need to make something happen—tonight," Max said, pulling up his phone as if inspiration might strike through his notifications.

"Agreed," Mei said, still tapping her foot to the beat in her head. She flipped open her notebook. "That was electric. We need to do something like that."

Max glanced over at her notes, squinting. "What makes stuff pop like that? It's gotta be fast. People don't stick around for long videos."

Mei nodded, already flipping pages. "Right. Short but with something that pulls people in right away."

Max paced, his thoughts bouncing as fast as his feet. "Like Xander Blaze's live event? Remember how the audience got to vote on what he did? That kept them hooked."

Mei's eyes lit up. "Yeah, but what if we push it further? Instead of just voting, the audience could control everything."

Max stopped in his tracks, grinning. "A real-life video game. They tell me where to go, what to do, and we make it total chaos."

Mei laughed, jotting it down. "That's perfect. I could even turn you into a video game character with makeup!"

"Love it! Collaboration for the win!" Max grabbed a nearby water bottle and started dodging imaginary obstacles. "Like, I'm dodging traps, collecting 'coins' or something, but they're the ones making me do it. Left, right, jump-"

"-Splat!" Mei laughed. "You *know* everyone's going to vote for whatever the most stupid thing is."

Max spread his arms. "Hey. I'm up for it!"

Mei giggled as he nearly tripped over the coffee table, before getting serious once more. "We'd need props, though. And backgrounds. Really make it look like you're in the game."

"Kaia?" Max asked.

"Yes! She could build the whole thing from scraps. Upcycled treasure chests, crates, whatever we need."

"And Piper and Lani could do the backgrounds. Their graffiti's sick!"

Max shot off a quick text.

Hey, got an idea that needs ur skillz. Up for
building real-life game props?

Mei leaned back, grinning as she watched Max spin around, hyped. "I can already see it—audience-controlled chaos, live interaction, and a real-life game that's totally us. We're not just making a video. We're making an event." She bit her lip "I think we've got a good idea. Now we just need to get lucky."

Max dropped onto the couch next to her, "Luck? We're making our own luck. This thing is gonna blow up."

MEI'S NOTES:
GOING VIRAL

Surprise is everything!

Whether it's a flash mob or a YouTube video, people love to be caught off guard. Start with something unexpected to grab attention.

Make people feel something

Lexie's dancers didn't just show off their skills; they connected with everyone. We need to make our audience feel involved, even if it's through a screen.

Keep it short, sweet, and chaotic

People don't have time to stick around for long intros. Hit them fast with something that's fun, quick, and easy to understand.

Basics first. Magic second.

Lexie's team rehearsed like crazy, but the best moments were spontaneous. As long as we've nailed down our core content, we can leave room for some chaos and fun.

Timing is everything
You can have the best video idea in the world, but if you don't post it when people are looking for it, it won't catch on. It's like how Lexie nailed the rooftop surprise just when the crowd needed something new. We need to hit trends at the right moment to really blow up.

Collaboration for the win!
The flash mob only worked because Lexie brought in different people with different talents. We need to collaborate more, whether it's props, backgrounds, or even letting the audience control the action!

Know who you're talking to
It's not just about making cool videos - it's about making videos your audience wants to see. Lexie's flash mob worked because it connected with everyone there, from kids to grandparents. We need to do the same with our content.

Be ready for luck—but don't count on it
Sometimes, things go viral because of timing or randomness. But the trick is to be prepared so when that luck hits, we're ready to make the most of it.

Viral moments are like Starlight Riot

Sure, the lead singer grabs attention, but without the band, he's just a lonely dude on stage. We need those viral hooks to pull people in, but it's our regular content that'll keep them coming back.

Storytelling is key

People love a good story - it's what pulls them in and keeps them hooked. Lexie's flash mob wasn't just dancing; it had a beginning, middle, and end. First, the statue came to life - bam, instant hook. Then the dancers built excitement as the crowd got involved, and just when it felt like it might end, they surprised us with the rooftop finale. It's like every good video: we'll need that setup, a bit of build-up, and a big moment that leaves people wanting more.

Be a comet

Do things slow, steady and properly, and soon we'll be shooting high above the sky.

Be the comet!

PART 12: THE LONG GAME: SUSTAINING GROWTH AND STAYING MOTIVATED

In which our intrepid heroes discover that some festivals linger in the air like magic, the tide carries more than just waves, and the night hums with the promise of something unforgettable.

57
GAME ON!

Stay inspired by your why
Set realistic expectations

Max and Mei huddled around a pile of props that Kaia's older brother, Jace, had helped transport to the community center where they'd be filming. The last time they'd been here, they'd only just started their YouTube journey, sitting on colorful beanbags to work out what they wanted to do with their channels.

Now, they were on the other side of the building—and their journey—hard at work transforming the center's huge fitness hall into a DIY video game set. The room looked like something straight out of *The Legend of Zelda's* latest game. A towering "ruined temple" dominated one wall, made from broken-down crates stacked and painted to resemble ancient stone pillars. Vines—actually old ropes Kaia had repurposed—hung from crumbling archways, giving the set an overgrown, abandoned look like a forgotten shrine.

On the floor, Kaia had spread out large, flat stones she'd made from foam mats, leading toward a treasure chest that wouldn't have looked out of place in Hyrule. The box, covered in Kaia's intricate gold designs, looked ready to hold absolutely legendary loot. In one corner, a weapon rack held a collection of swords and shields, all upcycled from discarded wood and pipes, mimicking the variety you'd find in a Zelda inventory.

Lines of painted masking tape had been used to create brickwork across the walls, and soft light filtered through high-set windows casting long shadows over the puzzles and obstacles before them. Dappled light spotted the floor just like forest shrines in the game. It felt as though Max and Mei could stride ten steps in any direction and immediately face a Bokoblin, or activate a Sheikah Slate to open the next challenge.

"This is looking epic," Max said, eyeing the finished props. "Kaia, you really nailed it with these."

Kaia grinned, brushing off her hands. "I had so much fun putting it together! Honestly, it's stuff like this that makes me love creating."

Mei was applying the finishing touches to Max's makeup, which she'd been vlogging about over the last week. She stepped back to admire her handiwork. "Have you ever thought about making your own YouTube channel?" she asked Kaia. "You could show people how to upcycle furniture just like this."

Kaia paused, considering. "I've thought about it, but I don't know... The idea of getting started is kind of overwhelming.

Max sat down on one of the crates. "Hey, you've already got what it takes—passion. That's how we all started. And we're here to help!"

Mei nodded. "Just don't expect a million views overnight."

Kaia smiled, looking around at the makeshift set. "I do love upcycling. And sharing that could be pretty cool."

Max jumped to his feet, picking up a foam sword they'd made for the challenge. "Look, none of us had a clue what we were doing when we started. Remember our first video, Mei? The lighting was a disaster, and the sound was so bad we could've been underwater."

Mei laughed. "Yeah, and we barely got any views. But we kept going because it was fun, and we figured it out along the way."

Max swung the foam sword dramatically, pretending to fight an invisible enemy. "Exactly. It's about enjoying the ride, right? The rest falls into place."

Kaia chuckled, watching him. "Alright, alright. I get it. I'll give it a shot. But I might need a crash course in editing."

"We're happy to help," Mei said with a smile.

"Don't get us wrong! Starting a channel isn't easy," Max grimaced. "But if you stay inspired by your *why*, you'll get there."

"My why?"

He glanced to Mei, then shrugged. "You know. Why you're doing this. Your passion."

"Besides," cut in Mei. "The first few videos don't need to be perfect. People love seeing the real process—mistakes and all."

Kaia raised an eyebrow. "So... like when Max tripped over that crate earlier?"

Max paused mid-swing, narrowing his eyes. "Hey, that was a tactical move."

The girls burst into laughter as they all got back to work.

—Five hours later—

Max collapsed onto the makeshift throne Kaia had built out of old pallets. "Okay, I'm officially dead."

Kaia laughed. "That happened two seconds into the adventure. Your subscribers did *not* care about your hit points... or your dignity."

Max held his head in his hands. "Don't remind me!"

"Left, left, LEFT!" the girls chanted, laughing.

At one stage the audience had spammed chat with the command on repeat, making Max run in circles until he almost threw up, and then made him climb a ladder. Needless to say, he didn't make it past the second rung.

The entire experience had been both as hilarious and chaotic as Max and Mei had hoped it might be, and the audience was already begging them to do it again.

"Our subscribers enjoyed my suffering way too much," Max moaned.

Grinning, Mei tossed her phone into her bag. "You loved it.

And the video was awesome."

Kaia wiped her hands on a rag, glancing at the props around them. "You know, even if no one ever sees this, today was a win. I've never had this much fun working on a project."

Max leaned forward, grinning back. "That's how you know you're on the right track. If you're having fun, your audience will too."

Kaia glanced at Max and Mei, their tired but satisfied smiles reflecting her own. "Okay, celebration smoothie?"

"Definitely," Max nodded, pulling out his laptop. "But let me do a quick cut of some of the highlights first? We'll get good watch hours on the longer video, but something short and sharp might have a better chance of going viral."

"Good idea. We'll pack up while you do it."

58
BE LIKE THE TIDE

Consistency over time

The team decided to grab their smoothies from the café where they'd first met Kaia, however after ordering them, they found the street bustling with activity. A crowd of volunteers, armed with gloves and trash bags, were gathering near the shore.

"What's going on?" Kaia asked, craning her neck.

Mei spotted a banner flapping in the wind. "Beach clean-up. Looks like they're getting ready to start."

Max glanced down the road, where the shoreline stretched out in front of them, littered with small pieces of trash left behind from the weekend. "Guess we know what we're doing next?"

Kaia smirked. "So much for a lazy afternoon."

They joined the volunteers, each picking up a bag and some gloves. The task ahead wasn't glamorous—plastic wrappers were tangled in seaweed, and bits of old food containers were wedged between rocks. Max groaned when he spotted an empty soda can floating in a tide pool. "This'll take forever."

Mei bent down, scooping it up. "Yeah, but if no one does it, the beach stays a mess, right?"

Max sighed but nodded. They spread out, slowly working their way across the sand, the rhythmic sounds of waves filling the silence. Each piece of trash they picked up was a tiny victory, though at first it seemed like they weren't making a dent.

Wiping her forehead, Kaia arched her back. "It's like trying to finish something that never ends!"

Mei chuckled. "Feels like it, doesn't it?" she said. "But check it out." She nodded over her shoulder.

Turning, they observed the clean beach behind them. And the growing line of volunteers. "That's wild," Max said. More and more were coming to help. "I guess that's how it goes with stuff like this. Little by little, it adds up. And if you stick with it... well, you actually start seeing progress."

Kaia chuckled, tossing another piece of trash into her bag. "Next you're going to say it's like starting that YouTube channel!"

Her voice deepened. "It's not much, but if you keep at it..."

"Hey!" complained Max. "I do *not* sound like that."

Mei snickered. "I thought it was pretty good. Though..." she eyed Kaia, "there's some truth to what you just said."

"Yeah, yeah. Get back to work," said Kaia. "And start telling me about YouTube. I heard there's a button you push that says 'Go Viral' when you upload?"

"Don't even start!" Max sputtered.

"Wouldn't that be nice?" Mei laughed. "But no, it's like this beach—individual videos don't seem like much, but over time, they add up. And the more you do it, the better you get at spotting what works."

"Exactly," said Max. "And the algorithm's like the tide."

Both girls turned to look at him. Mei pulled a face.

Max sighed. How could they not see it? "If you're consistent, the algorithm starts to notice, kind of like the tide. When it rolls out, it picks up whatever's there. If you toss one stick, sure, it might get carried out. But if you keep tossing stick after stick, the tide grabs them all. And the more you send out, the better your chances of those sticks reaching someone."

Mei and Kaia looked at each other.

"Huh. That actually kinda made sense," said Mei.

"Don't tell him, he'll get a big head," replied Kaia.

"Hey! I'm right here!"

They all laughed.

The bags slowly filled, and as the day wore on, the beach began to look cleaner, almost glowing in the late afternoon sun. Max dusted his hands as they reached the opposite end of the beach, looking back on what they'd done with pride. "It's crazy—one piece at a time doesn't feel like much, but if you keep at it..."

Mei grinned. "That's the key, right? Like the tide!"

59
START SMALL, DREAM BIG

Celebrate small wins
Plan for the long haul

As the beach cleanup wound down, the sun dipped lower, casting a soft glow over the sand. Max, Mei, and Kaia stood near the café, hands dusty but feeling accomplished. Volunteers milled around, chatting and hydrating, when someone called out, "Hey! Over there. Isn't that Starlight Riot?"

Max squinted toward a group near the shoreline. Sure enough, the band was helping toss bags of trash onto a growing pile.

"No way," Mei whispered. "They've been cleaning up this whole time?"

Kaia smiled. "Guess rock stars are good at more than just playing music."

One of the volunteers, starstruck but full of excitement, ran into the café and came back triumphantly holding a weathered acoustic guitar. When Starlight Riot came off the beach, he dashed over with a sheepish grin. "Any chance we could get a song?"

The lead singer laughed, grabbing the guitar to tune it. "Sure, why not?"

A strum echoed across the beach, drawing the attention of scattered volunteers. A small crowd began to form, the beach cleaners becoming an impromptu audience, some still holding trash bags and gloves. Max, Mei, and Kaia wandered closer as music flowed through the air.

"That's pretty cool," Max said, tapping his foot to the beat.

Many in the crowd texted friends, and before long, others trickled in, curious about the unexpected performance. A few of the beach cleaners set down their bags, pulled out their phones, and started filming.

"Ah, what the heck," the lead singer said. "Let's amp things up." He pulled out his own phone. "Geoff? Yep, bring the gear. Sound and stage." Before long, the band's crew arrived, holding cases of equipment. The impromptu concert was about to level up.

Word quickly spread. More people arrived, and soon, the casual guitar strumming had turned into a full-blown gig. Vendors from the nearby streets, hearing about the performance, showed up with their own stands. A group of cosplayers wandered over, dressed in costumes fresh from their weekly meetup. Max recognized several from the convention.

Even more people arrived. Among them was another person Max recognized. "Isn't that the dude who sold us our starting equipment?" he asked.

The assistant who had given them such good advice so long ago was setting up a stall selling DIY gadgets near the café entrance.

"Hey, Jake!" Mei called, walking over. "Fab eyeliner!"

"Thanks!" he replied with a wink. "Been following your channel. Picked up a few tips." He gestured around at his stall. "I got inspired when I saw what you did—I'm no YouTuber, but I decided to start my own business!"

They both high-fived him.

"It's not much now," he said, suddenly becoming embarrassed. "But one day I'll have my own shop."

"Nonsense," said Mei. "This is amazing! You made the first step! Without it, you'd still be stuck in that shop!"

He grinned. "Yeah, guess you're right. Celebrate the small things, right?"

"Uh huh," Mei nodded. "Cause without the small wins, you can't have the big ones."

Kaia looked around at what had quickly blossomed into a festival. The warm glow of the setting sun made everything feel alive. She smiled, her voice tinged with awe. "This really turned into something, didn't it?"

Max nodded, watching more people arrive, some setting up new stalls, others joining the crowd. "It's cool, right? To think this all started because someone asked a café for a guitar."

"Small wins, right?"

Max cocked his head. "I don't follow."

Mei laughed. "You must be rubbing off on me. Usually, you're the one doing the explaining! I just meant, it's like Jake the tech guy all over again. You might have a vision of something grand, but it's gotta start small. Like a festival growing out of someone giving Starlight Riot a guitar."

A woman in a bright yellow vest wove through the crowd, clipboard in hand. She paused beside different groups, chatting briefly before handing them a pen. People smiled, nodding as they signed their names on the clipboard.

"Who's that?" Max asked, pointing toward the woman as she approached.

Mei squinted. "I think she's the cleanup organizer. Looks like she's getting people to sign up for next year."

Sure enough, the woman soon made her way over, flashing them a friendly smile. "Hey there! We're already planning next year's beach cleanup. Would you like to sign up? We could use all the help we can get."

Mei glanced at Max before taking the pen. "Planning ahead, huh? That's smart."

The organizer nodded. "Absolutely. We've been doing this for years now, and every time we grow a little more. It's all about thinking long-term. If we keep showing up, the beach will just get better and better."

Max signed the clipboard and handed it back. "We'll be here. Same time next year?"

The woman laughed. "You got it."

She approached Starlight Riot next. After a brief conversation, the lead singer stepped back to the mic.

"Hey, everyone! Just wanted to give a shoutout to the organizers of this awesome event. We've signed up to come back next year, and hope you all will, too!"

The crowd erupted in cheers, and more people hurried over to the organizer's clipboard, eager to contribute.

Mei smiled. "Guess that's how you keep things going—always looking ahead."

Max nodded, watching as the festival buzzed around them. "It's not just about showing up once. It's about sticking with it."

The band played on. Starlight Riot's impromptu performance had turned into something far bigger than anyone expected, but it felt right—like a celebration of all the small wins that had led them here.

Max raised his new smoothie in a toast. "Here's to celebrating the small stuff... and growing whatever comes next."

Mei clinked her cup against his. "And to the long game. One step at a time."

Kaia just nodded; her expression unusually quiet.

60
THE SEED OF WHAT MATTERS

Adapt to trends but stay authentic

Kaia was somber as they walked through the festival. Though Max and Mei tried to cheer her up, eventually she sighed. "I've been thinking about my channel," she said. "Upcycling is fun. It's what I love. But maybe I should start with IKEA tutorials or something more popular. It's still furniture, right? And it would get me a ton of views."

Max frowned, exchanging a glance with Mei. "But that's not why you wanted to start your channel."

Kaia shrugged. "No, but... if it gets more views, doesn't that make it worth it? I can do the stuff I love later, once I'm established."

Mei opened her mouth to respond, but the words didn't come. Max rubbed the back of his neck. "I don't know... something about that feels off."

A vibrant display caught their eye. They turned to see Cuthbert, the plant, now in a sleek, colorful pot, sitting proudly at the center of a lively stall. Their conversation paused as they drifted closer. "Whoa," Max said, nudging Mei. "Looks like they went all out."

The stall was buzzing with energy. There were graffiti designs splashed across the booth, glowing plants under black lights, and a group of teens snapping pics in front of a photo booth filled with exotic plants. Crazy Mike was tinkering with a set of glowing cables while Cuthbert's owner greeted visitors with a grin. A couple of teenagers laughed as they posed with oversized plant-themed props, tagging their photos with the hashtag *#CuthbertCrew.*

"They weren't kidding about jazzing it up," Mei said, remembering the last conversation they'd had with Cuthbert's owners. "Look at the graffiti! They must have hooked up with that graffiti artist from the mural!"

Even Kaia brightened as she looked around. "Wait, is that... a charging station?"

Sure enough, there were small signs next to the pots reading "Charge Your Phone, Powered by Plants!" A few teens had plugged in their phones, chatting as they leaned against glowing chairs in what appeared to be a "Zen Zone" tucked away under the shade.

Crazy Mike spotted them and waved. "Hey, you three! Come check this out!"

They weaved through the crowd toward him. Mike pointed to the row of colorful plant pots on display. "Still the same smart pots we've been working on, just... with a bit more style now." He gestured to the photo booth. "People love snapping pics with the plants. Plus, we've got some cool prizes for the most creative posts."

Mei smiled. "You've definitely taken it up a notch."

Cuthbert's owner joined them, wiping his hands on his jeans. "Yeah, we have you to thank for that, partially."

"Really?"

He nodded. "We got chatting with that graffiti artist, bounced some ideas around... and things kinda snowballed. Figured if we were going to keep up, we had to do more than just sell pots. People want an experience now, something they can share."

Kaia tapped one of the pots, her face thoughtful. "But you didn't change what matters."

"Exactly," Cuthbert's owner said, nodding. "The pots are still the heart of what we do. But we're giving people new ways to connect with them. We've got plans for still more, too."

Crazy Mike grinned, clearly excited. "We're working on an AR experience—imagine pointing your phone at one of these pots and seeing the plant's growth cycle or little animations pop up!"

Mei glanced around at the buzzing stall, teens snapping photos, and the relaxed atmosphere in the Zen Zone. "You've found a way to keep things exciting without losing what made people care in the first place."

Kaia was quiet, her eyes flicking between the smart pots, the graffiti art, and the glowing Zen Zone. The energy of the stall was undeniable, but at its core, it was still about the plants, about something real. "That's it, isn't it?" she murmured.

Max cocked his head. "Had an idea?"

She nodded. "They didn't change what mattered—they just made it more fun to connect with. If I start chasing trends that don't fit me... I'll lose what made me want to do this in the first place."

Max and Mei smiled, both relieved to see her realize it for herself.

"If you lose what makes you... you, it won't work in the long run," said Max.

"Exactly," agreed Mei. "You can adapt, but you've got to stay true to your why."

When they moved on, Kaia had a spring in her step that hadn't been there when she arrived.

61
VIRAL

Use analytics to adjust, not obsess

The festival was winding down, but energy still buzzed in the air. Starlight Riot had wrapped up their impromptu set, and the makeshift stalls were slowly being packed away as people lingered around, soaking in the last moments of the day.

Max, Mei, and Kaia found a quiet spot near the edge of the crowd, their phones in hand. Their viral challenge video had been live for a few hours now, and the early results were coming in.

Max refreshed the analytics screen, a grin creeping across his face. "It's looking good. We're picking up steam."

Kaia leaned in, eyes lighting as she watched the numbers rise. "This is so cool! I can't believe it's happening in real time." She glanced at Mei. "I don't even have my own channel yet, and I'm already excited about your numbers."

Mei smiled, nudging her gently. "When you start your own channel, this is something you'll want to keep in mind. It's tempting to obsess over the analytics, but you've got to be careful."

Kaia looked puzzled. "Why? Isn't it a good thing to watch the numbers?"

Max leaned against a post, phone still in hand. "It's useful, yeah, but it can also be a trap. You don't want to spend all your time refreshing the page and chasing every little spike or dip. Just look at what's working—what kind of videos are getting the most engagement. Then put it down."

A smile tugged at the corners of Kaia's mouth. "So, I'm guessing refreshing the page every five minutes isn't the way to go?"

Max laughed. "Nah, it'll drive you nuts. Check it now and then, see what's working. But don't sweat every little dip."

Mei nodded, tucking her phone away. "Churro?"

Max looked around. "We'd have to be quick. I saw a food truck, but I think it's packing up."

Mei and Kaia exchanged glances, then sprinted in the truck's direction. "Last one pays the bill!" Mei called over her shoulder.

"Hey!!"

Twenty minutes later, they were sitting on crates finishing their churros—Max still grumbling about having to pay—when Mei's phone beeped. She ignored it to lick sugar from her fingers.

Kaia's phone beeped several seconds later. Kaia pulled it out, face lighting from the glow of her screen.

Max cocked his head, noting her frown, and then the soft chimes of more people getting text messages all around them. People were checking their phones, chuckling, and then showing friends, partners, and loved ones.

"What's going on?" asked Mei.

"Alien attack?" guessed Max. "No wait… zombies!!"

This time it was Kaia, not Mei, who rolled her eyes. "Um… you guys might want to check your YouTube channels."

"Oh no," muttered Mei. "Something broke, didn't it?"

Kaia's expression twisted into a nervous grin. "Yes… in a way."

"Crap!" Hastily wiping their fingers, Max and Mei reached for their phones.

Max had his open first. When he saw what had gotten Kaia's attention, his mouth dropped. "Oh."

Moments later, Mei was seeing the same thing. "Oh."

Kaia's lips curved into a broad smile. "Pretty amazing, huh?"

"Five hundred thousand," Mei whispered, voice barely audible. "No, six…"

"No, seven!"

They stood there, stupefied, as they watched their numbers climb. Their game inspired video had now hit *one million* views… and it was still climbing.

Max and Mei looked at each other. "Are we?"

"I think we are!"

They leaped from their crates, pumping fists in the air. "YouTube Superstars!!"

MEI'S NOTES:
THE LONG GAME

Stay inspired by the "why"
Like Max told Kaia, our passion for why we first started should be the driving force behind everything we do. Keeping this in mind will help us stay motivated, even when things get tough.

Set realistic expectations
Success doesn't happen overnight. Don't expect a million views immediately. Every big journey starts with small steps.

Consistency over time is key
Just like the beach cleanup, small efforts made consistently can lead to significant results. Regularly posting content will help grow our channels over time. Be like the tide!

Celebrate small wins
Every little achievement is worth acknowledging. These small victories build momentum and keep me motivated for the long haul. *LOL. Max says I have to write down that we need to celebrate the big wins too!!*

Plan for the future

Thinking ahead and setting long-term goals can keep us focused. Planning helps us know what video to make next, and keeps us on track for success.

Tactical move?

Apparently, tripping over a crate is now considered a "tactical move" - thanks for the laugh, Max!

Adapt to trends but stay authentic

Sure, chasing trends can get you quick views, but if it doesn't feel like *you*, what's the point? Stick to what you love - that's what your audience will connect with, and it's what keeps you excited to create.

Use analytics to improve, Not obsess

Analytics are useful for understanding what works, but obsessing over numbers can be distracting. I'll use them as a tool for growth, not as a measure of self-worth. Though, it was nice to see all those sweet, sweet zeros when we hit 1 million!! Arrrrrrghgghghghghghghg!

AUTHOR'S NOTE

Hey there, awesome reader!

First off, thanks for sticking with Max and Mei on their epic journey to YouTube stardom. I hope you had as much fun reading their story as I did writing it — and maybe picked up a few tricks to help you crush it on YouTube too!

Now, I should probably introduce myself... sort of. I go by Max Awesome, which isn't my real name (but let's be honest, it's way cooler). Why the pen name? Well, I figured if I was writing a book about making epic content, I needed a name that screamed legendary.

If you enjoyed YouTube Superstars, I'd love it if you could leave a review — it seriously helps more people find the book (and gives Max and Mei a better shot at world domination... or at least YouTube fame). Make sure you mention if you're starting a YouTube channel in the review! I'll be your first subscriber ;)

Stay awesome,

Max

www.ingramcontent.com/pod-product-compliance
Lightning Source LLC
LaVergne TN
LVHW022336060326
832902LV00022B/4069